"The book *What in the World Was God Thinking?* provides an excellent study that helped me understand God's kingdom, the current and future roles of believers in the kingdom, and my relationship to Jesus Christ. It is an insightful approach that has given me a fresh focus as a Christian. I heartily recommend it either for personal devotions or for a group study series."

—**D. Wayne Kellogg**, PhD, former chair of the Department of Animal Science, University of Arkansas

"Identity, who we are, why we are here, and how we are to get there are all basic questions about life. Getting those questions aligned with what God is doing and why leads to proper life alignment. Every now and then it is good to come up for air in our hectic lives and pause and consider where we are, what we are doing, and why. *What in the World Was God Thinking?* is a wonderful resource by which to pause and consider such questions. Whether you are a new Christian just getting started or one who has been on the road for a while, this book will help you get reoriented and well aligned with what God is doing with you and why."

—**Darrel L. Bock**, PhD, Senior Research Professor of New Testament Studies, Dallas Theological Seminary

"Today and throughout the ages, it has been intellectually viable to consider that life on earth could or does precede a timeless existence. Kirk Hartness provides a fresh and stimulating integration of God's instructions and assurances for how we should live. He stresses that there is no excuse for being an ignorant Christian. One does not need to concur with every nuance in this book to find it valuable. I recommend it as a challenging, reassuring, refreshing, and spiritually enriching commentary. It will make you think about the relevance of your goals and actions in this life."

—**Roland M. Smith**, EdD, Professor Emeritus,
University of Arkansas

"How many times have we heard the phrase, 'To put this in perspective . . . ?' What is ultimately most helpful to every Christian (and even the non-Christian) is to get an eternal perspective, to see God's plan and purpose for our lives. Author Kirk Hartness invites the reader to look beyond the narrow perspective of cultural religion and grasp the greater, deeper reality of what it means to be a member of God's kingdom through faith in Jesus Christ. *What in the World Was God Thinking?* lays out God's plan for not only our personal salvation but also our daily experience as members of His eternal Kingdom. By reading this book, you will receive a whole new perspective."

—**Dennis Hillman**, pastor, author, publishing professional

WHAT IN THE WORLD WAS GOD THINKING?

WHAT IN THE WORLD WAS GOD THINKING?

*Answering Life's Ultimate Questions
for Now and Eternity*

KIRK HARTNESS

credo
house publishers

Published in the United States by Credo House Publishers,
a division of Credo Communications, LLC, Grand Rapids, Michigan
www.credohousepublishers.com

ISBN: 978-1-625860-013-2

Scripture is taken from the New American Standard Bible®, Copyright
© 1960, 1962, 1963, 1968, 1971, 1972, 1973, 1975, 1977, 1995 by The
Lockman Foundation. Used by permission.

Editing by Michael A. Vander Klipp
Cover and interior design by Frank Gutbrod

Printed in the United States of America
First edition

CONTENTS

FOREWORD

This is an important book because it clearly defines and expounds a truth that is dominant in the Bible. That is, kingdom truth, and Kirk brings a fresh approach to understanding it. He takes us through some modern thinking, which finds us where we are, only to help us understand a true biblical view.

He comes to us with four years of college, four years of seminary, and 25 years of personal study of the Scriptures. Kirk has had a ministry as a Bible expositor and evangelist in both the United States and Central America.

The author helps us understand who we are and why we are here. He makes the Christian life an exciting venture. It's like discovering a very important secret, that is, where we fit into God's plan. Kirk helps us become oriented by clear biblical thinking. It is an excellent exposition of how we are related to the kingdom of God.

—Warren E. Bathke, PhD

INTRODUCTION

Have you ever sat down and reflected on the condition of the world around you? What do you encounter when you watch the news or listen to the radio on your way to work? Political strife, local crime, natural disasters, and other sorts of mayhem fill the headlines. So many people take a defeatist attitude, concluding with their hands in the air, "Life is tough, and then you die." Without doubt there's more than enough to be concerned about, as the economic, social, moral, and spiritual condition of the world seems to be spinning ever more out of control.

In light of all of the difficulties we encounter, have you ever wondered whether God even exists? And if He does exist, have you asked yourself what He was thinking when He created the world?

Many years ago a trilemma was stated in this way:

- If God exists and is good, He should want to do something to stem the tide of evil.

- If God is all-powerful, He could stop evil whenever He wanted.
- So either God is not good, He is not all-powerful, or He does not exist.

A cynical take on the existence of God, for sure. But if God does exist, if He is good, and if He is all-powerful, then what is this craziness we call human life really all about? What in the world was God thinking when He created the world and put people in the Garden of Eden? These are some weighty questions, questions that lead to the three most important ones we can ask:

- Where did I come from?
- Where am I going?
- Why am I here?

The ultimate answers to all three can only be found in God. He's the source of all we see, and He alone has the answers to the fundamental questions that define our existence.

"We are all travelers in this world. From the sweet grass to the packing house. Birth 'til death. We travel between the eternities," reflected Robert Duvall in the movie *Broken Trail*. Whether or not we like it, the moment we're born we embark on a journey. Each of us along the way is faced with these ultimate questions of existence. So what about you? Have you taken the time to reflect on the meaning of life and asked those three most important questions men and women can ever attempt to answer?

I'm a fan of the legendary folk artists Simon and Garfunkel, two of the more influential poet/philosophers of my youth (at least they were periodically philosophical). In their song "Patterns" you can catch glimpses of their thoughts, and perhaps echoes of thoughts we've all had. The song addresses life's felt emptiness. The writers perceive of life as a bunch of disconnected pieces to a puzzle, which they seek to assemble to make sense of the nonsense. They go so far as to compare their lives to that of a rat in a maze, an existence of scrabbling their way through an endless pattern that finally ends in death. In their minds life is out of control, and they're battered by events they didn't ask for or want.

Perhaps you've felt this way yourself. You lie in bed at night feeling as though all you can do is to follow your life's preset pattern, hurtling headlong into the future with seemingly little control over the events of your life. Or maybe you lie there mentally seeking to put together the pieces of the puzzle that's you.

How many pieces are in this puzzle? First there are the family pieces, then the relationship and job or career pieces, . . . and somewhere in the mix is that elusive God piece. The pieces are there, but they're scattered and seemingly defy organization into a meaningful pattern. Some are genetic, defining us physically, mentally, and even emotionally. Others have been put in place by others with whom we've come into contact. And then there's that odd-shaped little number called the spiritual piece. Does it really exist and, if so, where does it fit into my life puzzle?

I've frequently stated that we're all products of the things done to us, for us, and by us. While all of these occurrences affect us as individuals, in many cases these different factors make it seem as though the pieces of the puzzle actually belong in separate boxes. Life can be highly confusing and stressful. But our life experiences, and the ways in which we respond or react to them, all work together to create the puzzle of our life. What, in the final analysis, gives the puzzle meaning? Where's the pattern our lives are supposed to follow, and to what end?

In the areas of morals and values, pastor, church planter, and author Ralph Neighbour once observed that "many people acquire their values like loose change they pick up on the street." Some are planted there by parents, some by teachers, and others by people we find attractive as role models—such as philosophers or entertainers.

In some cases our values may even conflict with one another. Years ago I talked with a friend who was planning to vote for a president whose values were totally different from those he personally held.

What do you value? Where did you acquire your values? Do the values you hold lead to a consistent worldview that enables you to arrive at intelligent decisions and make sense of your existence? This book is designed to lead us through the process of answering these ultimate questions, as we look backward at our life and strain forward toward what that life may hold in the future.

CHAPTER 1

DETERMINING A REFERENCE POINT

"A finite point without an infinite reference point is meaningless and absurd."

—JEAN PAUL SARTRE

A s we discussed in the introduction, the ultimate questions of life face each of us. And as we journey every day we need to find a reference point, a fixed place in time and space that will give us an idea of where we are, where we've been, and where we're going.

If I direct you to go from point A to point B, you have to know the locations of both points relative to where you are, as well as to one another, in order to find your way. Without such immovable set points we'll never know how to get wherever it is we're going. So the question is this: for us as human beings, is there a reference point in the vast infinity of space where we can drop anchor? And, if so, what and where is it?

Before we get too far into this book we have to deal with the question of how we got *here* in the first place. To begin to answer this question, we'll look first into the Bible, way back to its beginning in the first few chapters of Genesis. As we do, many may wonder whether I truly believe Genesis 1–10 constitute real history. Do I as the author of this book really believe that God created the earth in seven days? Do I truly believe Adam and Eve were real people? Was there really a tree of forbidden fruit? A devil? Was there really a worldwide flood and an ark? Did Noah actually live and build the ark by himself? I want to deal with these questions briefly.

The question about the seven days of creation harks back to Genesis 1, where the author clearly states that God created the earth in six days and rested on the seventh. My reason for pausing here to consider the evolution vs. scientific creationism/intelligent design debate is that so many try to discredit the whole discussion by identifying the Genesis account as allegorical or symbolic rather than real. Sounds benign enough, but the crux of this issue is that most of the rest of the story of the Bible depends upon the veracity and accuracy of its first ten chapters. A short look at the debate might be helpful.

First, there's really no dispute between science and the Bible, as long as scientists stick to the facts. Science can't prove either that God does or doesn't exist. The goal of science is to observe and define the facts and then determine what they might mean and how they fit together. Scientists create theories to explain what they're observing. Whether or not the theory of evolution happens to be true is secondary to the question of how things came into existence. The problem isn't with the observation of facts or phenomena but stems from trying to attribute—or even force-fit—those indisputable facts into a particular set of philosophic presuppositions.

There are only two possible explanations for where everything in the universe came from. Either the universe evolved or it was created. There may be many variations on either theory, but there are no other basic, ultimate possibilities.

On the evolution side, many scientists tell we're the byproducts of an explosion of energy some fourteen billion years ago now called "The Big Bang." The energy organized itself into all types of atoms, molecules, gases, etc., ad infinitum. Over time these particles organized themselves into all that we see in the universe today. In this scenario there's no intrinsic organizing principle or intelligent organizer. Over time, so the theory goes, energy simply transformed itself into matter and the matter into all that we see, both the animate and the inanimate. The theory boils down to the assertion that we're all simply accidents of an explosion of energy and blind, random chance.

Based on this theory, the only "meaning" that exists is whatever we can delude ourselves into believing. Our inexhaustible search for relevance gropes around for something that might organize the chaos and provide us with a way to piece together the puzzles that are ourselves and our environs. But if secular evolutionary theory is correct, any attempt to find meaning is a form of self-deception.

It's interesting to me that one of the great struggles in human life, both today and continuously throughout history, is that frenetic, all-consuming quest for meaning and purpose. Yet the evolutionist has adopted a philosophy that renders everything meaningless and purposeless. Are we really to settle for the explanation (or non-explanation!) that we came from nothing, will go to nothing, and in the middle are left grappling about in a futile attempt to generate some kind of purpose that will allow us to push ahead? Are we really to attempt to bury our emptiness through panaceas like secular philosophy, psychology, drugs, alcohol, sex, materialism, or some other temporary diversion? If there truly is no purpose in life—no "aha!" on our horizon—why is it we can't just leave the question alone?

The only other alternative explanation is that there is an infinite God who created all that we see today. Because

He is all-powerful, He has provided the energy and design necessary to create and uphold everything that exists. Furthermore, because He is infinitely intelligent, He Himself is the organizing principle that keeps it all going.

Belief in God can certainly encompass some of the elements of the Big Bang theory since God is, by definition, power or energy and much more. For example, the Big Bang postulates that the universe began with a burst of energy that would have had to include light, even though there was no sun. Genesis 1 states that light was created before the luminaries (sun, moon, and stars). The believer would postulate that God is much more than infinite power and energy. He is infinite also in wisdom and knowledge. Belief in God can provide substantive answers to the big questions with which humans seem engineered to wrestle, such as purpose and organization. Evolutionary theory, sans a Creator, as an explanation for the origin of the universe can't do this.

The goal here isn't to launch a scientific defense of biblical creationism or what some call "intelligent design." However, I personally find the second explanation to be the only comprehensive theory to convincingly explain our existence. Belief in an intelligent Designer is easier to swallow than acceptance of the random nature of the secular "Big Bang." Some of the greatest minds in science don't even buy in to this.

Albert Einstein gave us the theory of relativity, and much of our knowledge of the universe flows from his work. Einstein's theory produced the notion that the universe is winding down and will eventually die as its energy expends itself. Einstein reasoned that if the universe will have an end it must also have had a beginning. And if the universe had a beginning, it must have had a Beginner. From there he concluded that there is nothing incompatible about belief in both God *and* science. Science can't definitively prove that God exists, but it can conclude that everything that exists reflects the handiwork of a master Designer. There's order and purpose in the creation, from the largest and most complex systems to the most miniscule components, that can only reflect the craftsmanship of an all-knowing Creator and Designer.

Even some credible evolutionary scientists are now crossing over and coming to the conclusion that an infinite power had to have created everything we see. In 1993 a symposium was held at Southern Methodist University in Dallas among three of the world's leading evolutionary thinkers and three others who held to special creation or intelligent design. One of the great admissions in the debate came when the lead evolutionist agreed that there was no definitive proof for the Big Bang, if that theory is taken to preclude God. So the evolutionists themselves had not adopted their positions based on facts but on faith!

As a philosophical aside, it's important to note that facts in and of themselves can't determine what we believe. Many in the scientific community would like you to believe that all of their conclusions about the origins of the universe are based on solid, evidentiary facts. That is, in my opinion, utterly ludicrous. I use evolution as an example, but I have seen this in many different areas of life. There are people of great intellectual ability and impressive education who have looked at the same set of facts and reached radically different conclusions.

How can this be? The reality is that what we believe determines how we interpret the facts. In a sense, particularly in the area of origins, we're free to interpret the facts to mean whatever we want them to mean. So one observer can look at the fossil record and see footprints of evolution and diversity where another sees only a path toward extinction. In this latter view, since there were many more life forms in the past then there are today, we're looking at a record of decreasing complexity.

One variation of evolutionary theory that has some traction in the Christian scientific community is that of theistic evolution. In this explanation the universe appears to be very old, and this may in fact be the case. Biblical chronology allows for only about six thousand years between Genesis 1 and the present. Theistic evolution is an attempt to reconcile the seven days of creation in Genesis 1 with the apparent age of the universe (currently, many within the scientific community propose that the universe is about fourteen billion years old).

In 2 Peter 3:8 the apostle writes, "But do not let this fact escape your notice, beloved, that with the Lord one day is like a thousand years, and a thousand years is like one day." Theistic evolutionists tend to subscribe to what is known as the "day/age" theory. They look at each day in Genesis 1 as a geologic age and therefore conclude that billions of years could be encompassed in a single day of creation. One of the major problems with the theory biblically is that the Hebrew language of Genesis 1 doesn't support this interpretation.

From a practical vantage point theistic evolution is a compromise position rejected by both secular scientists and special creation scientists. The secular scientists tend to view it as unnecessary, while the special creationists have other explanations that, from their perspective, satisfy the problem.

Certainly belief in a special creation by God is no more absurd than the evolutionary belief that everything came into being not only from nothing but with no underlying cause or source. In fact, belief in God provides more meaning and sense to the puzzle that makes up our existence than does the Big Bang. Evolutionary theory proposes a huge infusion of energy with no source of origin, an explosion from an unknown—or nonexistent—cause, followed by the transformation of that energy into inanimate and animate matter with no organizing force or principle.

Another group has examined and promotes the philosophy called theistic evolution. Proponents believe that God has used evolution as a part of the creative process in the universe. While I don't want to take a lot of time here explaining the relative merits and deficits of this theory, I will make an observation: Jesus believed in the historical Adam and Noah. The genealogies in Matthew and Luke trace the roots of our existence back to Adam and Eve. Paul believed in Adam as a real, historical person, as did Peter. Jesus, Paul, and Peter all pointed to various theological realities, such as original sin, judgment, and the re-purchase or redemption of humankind, by harking back to the stories of Adam and Noah. If you propose, as some theistic evolutionists do, that these ancient people and events are figurative or allegorical, you've removed the explanations for the theological underpinnings of the New Testament.

Evolutionary theory corroborates the conclusion of Henry David Thoreau as he looked at life: "The mass of men lead lives of quiet desperation." Life is difficult for most of us. In fact, it can frequently be characterized as a desperate chase to maintain existence and meaning in the midst of chaos that is only infrequently punctuated by moments of happiness and joy. As one professor told a friend of mine years ago, "Life is tough, and then you die." Isn't it fascinating that, according to the evolutionists, man has evolved to the point that he now recognizes the absurdity of his own existence and has developed a philosophy of hedonistic despair in an attempt to infuse life with meaning?

I am writing from the position of special creation and the belief that there is an infinite God from whom we derive our existence and in whom we find meaning. I am also writing from the position that God has spoken through the men who wrote the Bible and that the Bible contains the answers to the riddles of life and can organize the pieces of the puzzle we don't always know what to do with.

I want to set a proposition before you. In Scripture we see this: God is the eternal King of the universe, who rules over an eternal kingdom. Currently He is populating His kingdom with an eternal people created uniquely in His image and being equipped, ever more and more, to rule His kingdom at a future time.

CHAPTER 2

THE UNSEEN KINGDOM

The kingdom of God is an eternal reality. Some posit that God's kingdom came into existence with the creation of the world. This isn't the case. Since the kingdom exists wherever the King is, it has existed forever. God has always been God; He has never been other than what He is. Therefore He has always ruled over an eternal kingdom. King David captured this reality in Psalm 145:13, where he wrote, "Your kingdom is an everlasting kingdom, and Your dominion endures throughout all generations." Nebuchadnezzar, king of Babylon in the time of Daniel, also got the point. In Daniel 4:34 Nebuchadnezzar says,

> "But at the end of that period, I, Nebuchadnezzar, raised my eyes toward heaven and my reason returned to me, and I blessed the Most High and praised and

honored Him who lives forever; For His dominion is an everlasting dominion, and His kingdom endures from generation to generation."

We catch glimpses of what this kingdom looks like through the Prophets. The reader only needs to look at Ezekiel 1, Daniel 7, and the book of Revelation in the Bible to catch glimpses of the kingdom of God. It's a realm of unparalleled beauty and magnificence. There are many more windows in the Bible through which we can view this kingdom, but the passages mentioned above are good places to begin.

Each of the visions in these books speaks of God's authority. In the books of Ezekiel and Daniel He is pictured sitting on His exalted throne. Each vision also showcases God's worship-worthy power. Isaiah 6, a vision of God in His temple, should inspire us to awe and worship. Seraphim, each having six wings, hover around the throne. With two wings they fly and with two they cover their faces, unworthy as they are to look upon the Person of God. With their last two wings they cover their feet and bodies, signifying their unworthiness to be exposed to God. In worship they cry out with thunderous voices, "Holy, Holy, Holy, is the LORD of hosts, the whole earth is full of His glory" (v. 3). In Hebrews 12:28 the author asserts that we as Christians will receive "a kingdom that cannot be shaken." Yet in Isaiah 6 the prophet tells us that the foundations of the thresholds of

God's temple tremble at the voice of the Seraphim who cry out "Holy, Holy, Holy . . ." The sound is deafening as they peal forth their praise.

These visions tell us of wondrous creatures that populate God's kingdom. From eternity past magnificent creatures known in the Bible as angels, cherubim, and seraphim, created as servants of God, have populated His kingdom. Throughout the Bible, and possibly even independently of the revelation of Scripture, people have glimpsed these beings in their incredible beauty and power. Throughout Scripture we witness people falling to their faces in dread and awe upon encountering one of them. In some cases the angels had to stop those who saw them from worshiping them, though they were always viewed as powerful creatures not to be taken lightly. The modern depictions of chubby winged children with innocent faces are a far cry from the description of angels in the Bible.

Please take the time to peruse these passages for yourself. They give us a glimpse of what the kingdom of God looks like.

CHAPTER 3

THE UNSEEN BECOMES VISIBLE

IMAGO DEI

y human reckoning, around six thousand years ago God created the present heavens and earth. The earth we know today began with a spoken word from God. We're told that God engaged the chaotic mass of earth and water by separating these elements by a division or expanse; He also created an expanse or firmament between the waters on the earth and those above it. The Hebrew word translated "expanse" or "firmament" conveys the idea of a bright piece of precious metal, like gold, being pounded out into what amounts to a mirror. The idea is that the created things were to be a reflection of what was going on in the heavens, a kind of mirror image. The earth and all that was in it was to be a reflection of the invisible kingdom of God. Each and every created creature and institution is a reflection of some invisible reality present in the kingdom of God.

Moses goes on to tell us in Genesis 1 that God populated the earth with the birds of the heavens, the insects, the beasts of the field, the fish of the sea, and the creeping things that crawl on the face of the earth. God created everything we see in our world, both inanimate and animate.

However, on the sixth day God added a creature that was distinct from every other He had created in the heavens and on the earth. In Genesis 1:26 Moses wrote: "Then God said, 'Let us make man in Our image, according to Our likeness; and let them rule over the fish of the sea and over the birds of the sky and over the cattle and over all the earth, and over every creeping thing that creeps on the earth.'"

The Latin words *imago Dei*, as applied to Genesis 1, are themselves a translation of the Hebrew and mean "the image of God." God created humans as the pinnacle or apex of His creation, and He inscribed us with His own image or likeness. No other creature can make this claim. This distinction doesn't apply to cherubim or seraphim or to the other angels. Remember that every created thing is a reflection of some reality in God's kingdom. Humans were created as a reflective image of God.

Let's look at another scriptural example. In Hebrews 1:3 the author describes Jesus as "the radiance of [God's] glory and the exact representation of His nature." I want to focus on two aspects of this verse. The first is the word "radiance." Visualize a light shining in the darkness. Sometimes you can see what looks like a halo or a glow around the bulb. This is its radiance. When the author of Hebrews depicted Jesus as the "radiance" of God's glory, he was referring to this idea of shining. If you want to know what the glory of God looks like, the radiance that shines from Him, all you need to do is look at Christ.

The second concept is "exact representation." In the Greek this is one word we can transliterate as *karaktar*. Look familiar? We derive our English word "character" from this word. In everyday life *karaktar* referred to an image stamped into something. For example, when a king had coins made he would have his face stamped or imprinted upon them. We do the same thing today when minting coins. In the Greek these images are referred to as *karaktars*. The author is telling us that Jesus is the "exact representation"—the "spitting image," if you will—of the nature or substance of God—the image or likeness of His Father.

Are you beginning to understand a little of what God was thinking when He created Adam and Eve? He was making living, breathing sons and daughters as representations of Himself. The image and likeness of God are bestowed only upon humans, and this is a gift of unimaginable worth. By crafting humans in His personal image and likeness, God created us to mirror Himself. We were created to be physical, moral, and spiritual representations of the invisible God in heaven; as such we're the pinnacle of God's creative work on earth.

Let's look a more closely at the image God implanted in us. What, more specifically, is the image and likeness of God? In what way or ways are we created to reflect Him?

We know that God exists in three persons: Father, Son, and Holy Spirit. Humans are created in a corresponding three-part image: each of us has a mind/soul, a body, and a spirit, each of which corresponds to a different Person of the Trinity.

Let's explore another aspect. Have you ever wondered about the origin and implication of our emotions? We experience love, joy, anger, disappointment, fear, envy, and a host of other "feelings." Where did these come from? In Galatians 5:22–23 Paul identifies the fruit of the Spirit as love, joy, peace, patience, kindness, goodness, faithfulness, gentleness, and self-control. If our emotive side is a fruit the Spirit wants to produce in our lives, isn't it reasonable to assume these emotions are characteristic of God Himself? Scripture makes it clear that God—in conjunction with being loving, patient, just, etc.—is also angry and jealous. Our feeling side is an authentic part of God's image in us.

CHAPTER 4

GOD'S PURPOSES AND PLANS FOR HIS PEOPLE

Why did God imbue us with these characteristics? He instilled these qualities within us so that we can respond to Him, appreciate Him, enjoy Him, and glorify Him. He wants us to be able to look at life through His eyes and hear it with His ears. He also did this so that He in turn can enjoy—can take delight in—us. When God created Adam and Eve, He implanted within them His own image as potential. God gave people an interesting task when He created them. He called finite creatures to attempt to both comprehend and reflect the attributes of a God who is infinite in every way.

Remember that Adam and Eve were immortal (deathless in terms of their physical bodies) when God created them. Had they not fallen into sin they would have had eternity here on earth to contemplate all that God is and means to us. The fall made us temporal (we now live in time) and temporary (we now have time limits, at least in terms of this present existence). Furthermore, the fallout from the fall has twisted us spiritually and emotionally, distorting our ability to comprehend and reflect upon (these two activities together equate to glorifying) God. One of the works of the Holy Spirit is to restore in us this two-pronged ability. This will not be accomplished in our earthly lifetime, but we'll have all eternity in the ultimate manifestation of the kingdom to revel in His beauty and goodness.

One of our greatest joys for us as parents is to see our children grow into mature, moral, responsible adults. This is a source not only of joy but also of untold comfort and pride. When I watch my son engaging with his wife and daughter I'm overjoyed. I see a young man who has learned what it truly means to be a man and to faithfully carry out the responsibilities of functioning as an adult, a husband, and a father. My wife and I are greatly blessed. In fact, all six of our children are walking with God and seeking to live out the implications of bearing His image in the world. What a privilege to see all of our children maturing and becoming what, and who, God wants them to be! God takes the same joy in our progress as we incrementally become more and more like Christ.

God created us, yes, but to what end? According to the account in Genesis 1–3, we were created to be His children. He is our Father in a very direct way. In this we are different from the angels, whom God created to be His servants (the word *angel* means "messenger"). There are different classes of these angelic beings described in the Scriptures. God created cherubim, seraphim, angels (used not in the generic sense but as a specific kind or category of messenger), and other beings to function as His servants and to carry out His will in the universe. However, when God created humans His goal was radically different. God was, and is still today, building a family for Himself.

First and foremost, we were created for fellowship with God. The declaration that we were created in His image and after His likeness appears already in Genesis 1. We bear the stamp of God's identity in our bodies, minds/souls, and spirits. When God says in Genesis 1 (we're overhearing a conversation from within the godhead!), "Let us make man in Our image, after our likeness," He is voicing His determination to craft us in exact correspondence to Himself—as exact representations, though finite in our attributes. Confirmation appears in Hebrews 1, where the author describes Jesus as "the radiance of His (God's) glory and the exact representation of His nature." The single word translated "exact representation" is, again, the English rendering of the Greek *karaktar,* from which we get our English *character.* The idea, as we've seen, is that of an image stamped into or imprinted upon a coin; a ruler may do this to remind the people who rules the land. Jesus is the "spitting image" of the Father. If you want to see what God looks like, look at Jesus.

When God created humankind, before the fall recounted in Genesis 3, He made them in the same form as Christ Himself—as *exact representations* of His nature. The image wasn't mature; that process requires time, education, and experience. Jesus Christ, as we know, is the unique, only begotten—as in generated or "born," not created—Son of God. He is God's child, albeit in a different sense than we are. And He is representative—the mold or model, if you will—of what God intended for humankind.

God wanted children whom He could love and with whom He could interact. He fashioned for His own glory and delight the human family to be a material reflection of the invisible reality of the interrelationships with the godhead (you may be more familiar with the term "Trinity"). Men, women, husbands, wives, marriage, and children—all of these temporary constructs were designed to point us in the direction of intimacy both within and with the divine. In Genesis we find God strolling through Eden, engaged in conversation with Adam and Eve. And in the New Testament

Jesus enjoyed perfect fellowship with God; the Gospel writer and apostle John makes clear that this provides the paradigm of what God wants to have with each of His children. The Father longs to talk with us, to love us and be loved back by us; He longs to be honored, glorified, and praised by us; and so on (see John 14:20, 23; 17:22–23.). He has seen fit to bestow upon *us* the ultimate honor and respect by creating us as His mirror images and desiring intimacy with us. What greater honor could be possible for a created being?

Second, God created us to rule the earth, to function here as His vice-regents, to govern the earth *through us*. In Genesis 1:26–28 God states His intention for us to subdue the earth and rule over it. In other words, He wants us to bring the earth into order and then govern all created things according to the blueprint of His design and on the basis of His delegated authority. According to Wikipedia the word *regent* derives from the Latin *regents*, which means "one who reigns." This is both an informal and a formal title assigned to a temporary, acting head of state in a monarchy. Thus, we are God's regents on the earth, called to faithfully follow his commands as we understand them from the Bible.

CHAPTER 5

GOD'S WAY OF GROWING CHILDREN

In Genesis 2 we read that God planted a garden we know as Eden. Have you ever asked yourself why God designed Eden and placed humans in it? We find that Eden had several purposes.

First, it was designed as a perfect place to live, a self-sufficient microcosm containing within itself everything necessary for human well-being Genesis 2:9 puts it this way: "Out of the ground the Lord God caused to grow every tree that is pleasing to the sight and good for food; the tree of life also in the midst of the garden, and the tree of the knowledge of good and evil." God created it to be a home for Adam and Eve where they could be sustained and nourished, where they could find happiness, fulfillment, and contentment.

Remember that God created the entire earth, but the Garden of Eden was special, distinct from the rest of the world at that time. Take a moment to envision a human garden and then reflect to the best of your imaginative ability upon what a garden God had specially created might have looked like (feel free to imaginatively indulge your other four senses as well).

The garden, at least in our limited imaginary iteration, featured trees, flowers, vegetables, grass, ornamental shrubs—everything imaginable for the first couple's physical and aesthetic enjoyment. Notice that verse 9 specifies that the garden contained plants that were both pleasing to look at and good for food—fruits, vegetables, grains, and nuts ideally suited to the nutritional needs of humanity. So the Garden of Eden was both sensually fulfilling and utilitarian, a place of incredible beauty that perfectly provided for the needs of Adam and Eve. Had they continued in fellowship with God, this location would also have housed their descendants.

Second, the garden was a location for work. Does is surprise you to learn that even before the fall God provided tasks for the first humans to accomplish? We may be sure these weren't "busy work" but meaningful and fulfilling accountabilities through which Adam (and later the rest of us) could channel his energy, passion, and creativity. In Genesis 2:15 we're told that God placed people in the garden in part to cultivate it (verse 5 even states that God delayed the entrée of plants until two prerequisites—rainfall and someone to work the ground—had been put in place). Genesis 1 and 2 describe God Himself at work creating the universe and all that is in it. God is at work, and we are His image bearers; ergo, work is an integral part of God's plan for us.

But work is more than a manifestation of God's image in us. Accountability helps us develop a sense of responsibility, a necessary component for leadership development. Furthermore, work develops in us pride of "ownership" and a gratifying sense of accomplishment. The work of our hands—and eyes and hearts . . .—is a creative outlet whereby we can take legitimate pride in God's having entrusted to us the ability to perform a job and do it well. Culminating the account of each day of creation, Genesis 1 includes a statement that God looked with satisfaction upon His own work and pronounced it good. God took pride and found satisfaction in His creation. Those of His image bearers who seek to exist without working are at cross-purposes with God's plan for human lives.

In Genesis 3:8 we read that Adam and Eve "heard the sound of the Lord God as he was walking in the garden in the cool of the day." The implication is that God had walked in the garden before, that this was a part of His daily routine with the first couple. When Adam and Eve heard His footsteps they were neither surprised by His presence nor ignorant of His identity. God was there to meet with His children and, as always, to parent them.

On that fateful day when Adam and Eve disobeyed God, however, He asked where they were—not because He didn't know but in acknowledgment of their futile attempt to conceal themselves from Him. Previously they had approached Him freely, anxious to enjoy His companionship. Now there was a change in the relationship. They were uncharacteristically holding back, hiding from God when they should have been running up and embracing Him as Father. Adam and Eve were created perfect, not in the sense that they were unable to sin but that they had no physical or mental defects. However, they were also created innocent—naïve, if you will—clueless about the concepts of obedience or even of the reality of good and evil. They, and we, were created for fellowship with God; He utilized the time spent in their company to develop His relationship with His children and to instruct them in His ways.

Fourth, In Genesis 2:16–17 we read that "The Lord God commanded the man, saying, 'From any tree of the garden you may eat freely; but from the tree of the knowledge of good and evil you shall not eat, for in the day that you eat from it you will surely die.'" What were the purposes of these two specific trees? God deliberately singled them out as unique in the garden from all of the other vegetation.

Those trees were created to develop the volition, or will, of Adam and Eve. Remember that God has a free will, meaning that He can do anything and everything He desires, so long as it's consistent with His nature. Once again, because Adam and Eve were created in the image and likeness of God they too were endowed with an unrestricted will. God could have created the first humans as living robots, capable only of unquestioning obedience. In that case, however, He would have simply created another type of servant. But true love can be expressed only when the recipient *chooses* to love back. God doesn't simply want children He can love and with whom He can share His gifts. He wants children who will, volitionally and of their own account, love, adore, honor, and respect Him. This love and respect are genuine only when they're freely offered, when they proceed from the recognition of and profound appreciation for who God is and what He has done for us.

The presence within humankind of a will was also intended to instill obedience and respect. One can't love someone they don't respect, and they can't respect someone they don't fear (as in revere or reverence). The threat of discipline hung over the first couple, although Adam and Eve were most likely unaware of the full implications of obedience and death when God spoke His original commands to them. They were warned that they would surely die if they ate of the wrong tree. Faith is at the very heart of obedience, and obedience is a necessary part of learning to lead or rule. Obedience is also an integral aspect of loving someone.

Let's take a moment to reflect on some of the words of Jesus Christ in John 14. In verse 15 He says, "If you love Me, you will keep My commandments," going on in verse 21, "He who has My commandments and keeps them is the one who loves Me; and he who loves Me will be loved by My Father, and I will love him and will disclose Myself to Him." In verses 23 and 24 our Lord adds, "If anyone loves Me, he will keep my word; and My Father will love him, and we will come to him and make our abode (home or dwelling place) with him. He who does not love Me does not keep My words." Do you see the tight connection between love and obedience? You simply can't have one without the other. Like two sides of the same coin, love is revealed in obedience and obedience is evidence of love.

God created the special trees in that garden to prepare Adam and Eve, and their children, to be sons and daughters qualified to act as leaders in his kingdom. A person who won't follow can't lead. To what degree do you respect "armchair quarterbacks"? These are the people who, although they may never have played the game, are constantly trying to call the plays and second-guessing the decisions of those officially charged with calling them. Similarly, in the military the most respected officers are the battle-tested. The troops under these commanders are aware that they've been in the trenches. In fact, in any sport or endeavor those who've played the game or had the firsthand experience are much more likely to be respected.

One of the problems in today's culture is that pastors and politicians are unable to personally relate to the life experiences of small business owners, factory or office workers, or stay-at-home parents. Still, many feel entitled to counsel their constituents on the nitty-gritty ins and outs of how they need to live, operate their companies, and spend their money. They tend to overlook the reality that experience begets integrity, which in turn engenders respect.

A warning was given to our original forebears regarding the tree of the knowledge of good and evil: "In the day that you eat of it, you will surely die." What did this mean? We now know that Adam and Eve chose to eat from this and that by their disobedience they plunged our race into death and misery. But when did they die? Genesis relates that Adam lived to be over 930 years old. How does this square, we might ask, with the forewarning that Adam and Eve would die (no time factor specified) when they ate from the tree? If God is true to His Word, we might conclude (on the assumption that the lack of a time reference equated to immediate) that Adam had to have died that same day. The truth is that in a sense he did: when he ate of the tree, Adam in a real sense died spiritually to God and to the life of God. From that day forward all men and women have been stillborn, spiritually speaking—spiritually cut off from God unless God opens a way back to life.

Remember back to our discussion of God's original purposes in creating us. We were created in His image and likeness for the purposes of fellowshipping with Him (which includes glorifying and delighting in Him) and ruling over the creation. Everything God put into the Garden of Eden was designed to develop Adam and Eve, and their descendants, for these purposes. However, our first parents failed, thereby consigning their, and our, race to meaninglessness and death.

It's vital for us to note, however, that the curses in Genesis 3 are temporal in nature, dealing primarily with life on this earth and the problems we face in the here (space) and now (time)—recall that both space and time are temporary constructs applicable only to the earthly phase of our eternal existence. The uncertainties and frustrations of life, along with pain, suffering, disease, depression, and all of the other ills from which we suffer are direct results of the curse. However, God did pave the way to hope after our first parents fell into sin.

CHAPTER 6

A DOOR AND A WAY CLOSED

I n Genesis 3:22–24 we read, "Then the Lord God said, 'Behold, the man has become like one of Us, knowing good and evil; and now, lest he stretch forth his hand, and take also from the tree of life and eat, and live forever . . . therefore the Lord God sent him out of the garden of Eden, to cultivate the ground from which he was taken. So He drove the man out; and at the East of the Garden of Eden He stationed the cherubim and the flaming sword which turned every direction to guard the way to the tree of life." Every time I think of these verses I hear in my mind a giant door clanging shut and the voice of God crying out, "You shall not enter this way again."

As you'll recall, there were two trees in the garden set apart for God's purposes: the tree of life and the tree of the knowledge of good and evil. When Adam and Eve sinned, the tree of life remained; the potential for eternal life was intact, beckoning any who might eat of its fruit. Yet an angel had been stationed at the gate to bar the way to that tree—that means of access to eternal life, it seemed, was closed and closed forever.

Earlier in Genesis 3 we read of the curses God levied against the characters in the drama of the fall. The curses are uniquely suited to the specific sins of each individual involved. The serpent had evidently been one of God's greater—or at least more canny—creations. In Genesis we read that the serpent was craftier than any other beast God had made. The word here translated "crafty" can mean subtle, shrewd, sly . . . or prudent. The idea is one of nimble intelligence. Because of the nature of his sin in tempting the first couple, the serpent was consigned to crawl on his belly and eat dust. He was relegated to being despised, an object of contempt and fear.

Eve had been created as a helpmate to her husband, one who was to come alongside him as a friend, lover, companion, and counselor. She was also to be a mother of their children and the steward of their home. Her desire in yielding to the temptation had been, at least in part, to outdo and one-up her husband. As a result, Eve was cursed in two ways: she would give birth to children in pain, and she would no longer be in a divine partnership with Adam. Eve, and all women since, was penalized in her area of fruitfulness, the bearing of children, and the area of relationship with Adam. From that point on the woman was consigned both to desire to control her husband and to be forever dominated by him.

God had created Adam to be the head of the created order. However, in his sin with Eve he became a passive participant. He knew God's command concerning the tree because he had heard it directly from God. But instead of exercising leadership in the situation he passively followed the initiative of his wife in doing what God had expressly forbidden.

Adam's sin both of shrinking back and transferring the blame for the fall to Eve was punished in at least two ways. First, he faced the prospect of a life of tedium and frustration in his work, doomed to be forever planting, cultivating, and weeding, trapped in an endless cycle of sameness, continuously at the mercy of proliferating thistles and repeating destructive weather patterns. The crops would be threatened by weeds, drought, blight, insects, cold, and heat. There would be no security and no predictability in his labor.

Second, he was cursed in his relationship with his wife, and ultimately with his children. Instead of a comfortable partnership with Eve, Adam was relegated to a tense relationship in which his wife would be forever seeking control, which he in turn would resist through domination.

Why did God close the gate to the garden after expelling Adam and Eve? The answer is that, had they proceeded to eat of the tree of life, they would conceivably have lived forever in sin and under its curse, separated eternally from the life of God and the fellowship for which He had created them. Which raises in our minds another *Why?* God explained in Genesis 3:23: "Lest they eat from the tree and live forever." God's intent was that Adam and Eve *not* live in an eternal state of separation from Himself. Their expulsion from the garden was an act of both justice and mercy. God had a plan in place to restore humanity to full fellowship with Himself.

Envision for a moment the 1993 movie *Groundhog Day*, in which the main character is trapped in a kind of time warp, reliving the same day over and over again. In a sense, if God had not barred access to the tree of life, Adam and Eve might have forever languished under these curses, plodding along year after year with neither an end nor hope on the horizon. The futility, pain, anguish, and aggravations of life might have recycled endlessly, year after year, forever.

This wasn't God's plan, and something had to be done. God's solution was to expel the pair from the garden and block the way back so they could never return. In essence, God put a triple lock on the east gate: two cherubim and a flaming sword. The door to Eden, to kingdom privilege and to eternal life, was slammed shut and secured with impregnable locks. *This way* back to sonship and dominion was forever barred.

Yet already at that point God met them with a glimmer of grace and an offer of hope—in and through His very act of judgment. Already then their punishment entailed the onset of the process of physical death. They would endure angst and discouragement and would experience the grief of separation from those they loved as, one by one, inexorably and incrementally, death began to snatch them away. They themselves would eventually die and be separated from those loved ones still alive, who in turn were bound to follow later. This consequence of the fall continues for all of humanity to this very day.

So where is the grace, and where the hope in the midst of so disastrous a situation? There remained the prospect that God might arrange for a new way back to Himself—for Adam and Eve and for all their progeny.

We were created for life, for fellowship with God, and for the purpose of governing under His leadership. Now we had been consigned to death and separation from God, adrift and barred from the very purposes for which He had fashioned us. God's Plan A for our sonship and dominion— the plan wending its way through the garden on the trek to kingdom life—remained forever closed off. A second gate or door needed to be thrown open, an alternative route through which God might fulfill His plans in us and for us. The good news: God has indeed opened that new way!

CHAPTER 7

A NEW DOOR AND A NEW WAY

The first book of the New Testament is the Gospel according to Matthew, and the first and longest recorded sermon of Jesus, the Sermon on the Mount, is set early in this account of Jesus' life (Matthew 5–7). It's interesting that in His first recorded sermon Jesus speaks of entering the kingdom through another gate or door. In Matthew 7:13–14 Jesus has this to say: "Enter through the narrow gate; for the gate is wide and the way is broad that leads to destruction, and there are many who enter through it. For the gate is small and the way is narrow that leads to life, and there are few who find it."

Christ speaks of two gates, two ways, and two destinies or destinations. In this important sermon early in his ministry, Jesus announces that something new is happening. The slamming of the gate to Eden in Genesis 3 cast all subsequent people into hopelessness from the time of their birth. Jesus announces the provision of another door. Let's look at the two gates as He describes them.

THE WIDE GATE AND THE BROAD WAY

Jesus cites the wide gate, ironically using it as motivation for opting to enter its narrow counterpart. Remember the earlier discussion regarding the Garden of Eden and its barred gate? Since the fall we've all been, spiritually speaking, stillborn, dead to God from our first breath. Despite an inborn yearning for God, we struggle futilely to reach Him. We're swept along in our inherited sin natures by the crush of the crowd elbowing its way through that wide gate in its hurry to travel the broad road: the road Christ warns us leads straight to destruction.

Think back to the beginning of this book and the quotation from the movie *Broken Trail*: "We are all travelers in this world. From the sweet grass to the packing house. Birth 'til death. We travel between the eternities." Like it or not, we're on a journey, traveling a road of life from the moment we're born. Lyrics from Simon and Garfunkel resonate with this theme:

From the moment of my birth
To the instant of my death,

There are patterns I must follow
Just as I must breathe each breath.

Like a rat in a maze
The path before me lies,
And the pattern never alters
Until the rat dies.

We're given one life and one opportunity to live it. Simon and Garfunkel may have been a bit deterministic in their outlook, but too many can relate to their depiction of a predetermined, hopeless course. While it's true that we're all born already in motion along our life's course, there are many twists, turns, and unexpected opportunities ahead of us. We have real choices to make. Remember that God created us in His image and likeness, and this includes the prerogative of choice. Also remember that true choice entails the ability to opt for inappropriate, ineffective, bad, or immoral choices. If all of our options were positive we could not, by definition, exercise real freedom of choice.

At any given point in time the circumstances of our lives, and the way we react to them, equate to the cumulative total of things that have been done by us, to us, and for us. At birth we're provided with parents and a genetic mosaic. Our parents have the early obligation to feed, clothe, bathe, and guide us into life. How well they've done their job is, in some respects, revealed in the way we conduct ourselves in our own lives. Parents do things to us and for us. Some are better than others, but none is perfect. The same is true of others we meet: the things they say and do will impact us in various ways. I don't believe in chance pairings or encounters; God places people in our path so that in large and small ways the individuals with whom we come into contact will have an impact on us—and we on them.

In a very real way we're all born already entering the wide gate and traveling the wide way. The reason we don't recognize this as the path to destruction is that so many are traveling with us, and we're all headed in the same general direction. Religion, philosophy, psychology, and so many other aspects of life are all touted on this road. It's easily traveled because it's wide; as long as we keep moving in the same direction without impeding the flow of traffic we won't encounter resistance from anyone else. And we find it fairly easy to circumnavigate apparent obstacles. The road is wide enough that we can just skirt the potholes or pitfalls. After all, there are multiple explanations for the human condition.

Some view all religions as alternate roads to God. If this is the case, it doesn't matter which you choose to follow. On the wide road no particular religion makes any critical difference. Any will do; in fact, having no religion at all is a viable option. And if the religions are irrelevant, ineffective, or on the wrong track, meaning and purpose might be found in any or all of the possibilities out there.

If relevance can be found anywhere, why are so many in despair? Why is Prozac® the number one drug prescribed in the United States? If all roads lead to God and all dogs go to heaven, why do we struggle so frenetically just to feed ourselves and stay alive? Why do we grapple with identity and purpose? Where did the impetus for this struggle even begin? Maybe, just maybe, there *is* something to those curses levied against Adam and Eve in Genesis 3.

The fact of the matter is that we all have a sneaking suspicion we're on the wrong road. The Bible tells us that God has implanted that nagging disquiet in our hearts. In the Old Testament book of Ecclesiastes, chapter 3 verse 11, the Teacher (Solomon) declares that God "has made everything appropriate in its time. He has also set eternity in [the human] heart, yet so that man will not find out the work which God has done from the beginning to the end." Blaise Pascal put it this way: "There is a God shaped vacuum in the heart of every man which cannot be filled by any created thing, but only by God, the Creator, made known through Jesus."

Most humans intuit this deep inside. Whether we're wealthy or destitute, successful or miserable failures, we feel the void. Yet how can we identify it for what it is? Our dis-ease is the yearning for God implanted within each of us by our Creator. The entire time we're trekking along on life's journey we sense a need to turn around, to backtrack and pick up that fork in the road we must have missed somewhere along the way. But the current seems to pull us along in spite of ourselves; the broad road, we realize, was engineered for one-way traffic, for going with the flow.

Christ warns that the wide road leads to destruction; as we humans walk that road God plants warning markers in our souls, urging us to seek Him. The Greek word for "destruction" or "destroyer" is *apollyon*, one of several names given to Satan or the devil. So many of us can look at our lives and see a trail of emptiness and destruction. By way of example, fully half of all marriages in the United States end in divorce. Many who've tried marriage multiple times find themselves bewildered, depressed, and disillusioned.

Our children are in open revolt as they too seek to fill the God-shaped void, in their case frequently with popular music and vulgarity—not surprisingly, without finding peace. Second only to accidents, the leading cause of death in young people in their teens and twenties is suicide. These statistics aren't made up or fudged. They come from the American Center for Disease Control and Prevention. (See Centers for Disease Control and Prevention, CDC 24/7, Saving Lives and Protecting People, online). Go figure. At a time when life should be filled with hope and optimism, it's spilling over with despair and depression for so many of our young people.

By and large we're disappointed in the way our lives are playing out, ultimately arriving at the disconcerting conclusion that nothing we try really satisfies. We think love will infuse life with meaning, but love fades. We think work will fill the void, but the daily grind or the rat race—however we characterize it—leaves us burned out and disillusioned. We seek to anaesthetize life's pain with liberal doses of philosophy, psychology, religion, drugs, alcohol, sex, or any number of other things that are touted as panaceas. We seek diversion through entertainment, hoping to get our minds off the struggle. But in the final analysis we lie on our beds at night still trying, as futilely as ever, to piece together that puzzle that is us. We can almost feel the destruction coming, even glimpsing hints of it in our lives right now. The promise and optimism that kept our younger selves going is being inexorably replaced by the quietly insistent conclusion that "this is the way it is—and it's *all* there is!" Yet deep inside we know this can't be true. There has to be another way.

Let's backtrack to our discussion of that broad way. What are its characteristics?

The broad way is well traveled. The majority of people are on this garishly lit thoroughfare, so much so that it would be easy to miss the modest narrow road entirely.

We're creatures who like to belong, and the popularity of this expressway provides the reinforcement we think we need to verify that we're moving in the right direction. The broad way looks like Easy Street, with no apparent resistance and relatively few obstacles.

The worldly person will have no difficulty finding support and confirmation along the journey. If they like philosophy, they'll find plenty of companionship. The same can be said about psychology, religion, and so forth (virtually any field of discovery or fantasy has its adherents). All alike on the broad road are moving in the same direction, so it will be easy to find others who will walk alongside and in agreement with them. The broad road is the way of the world; those who walk it will never find themselves at a loss for companionship.

THE NARROW GATE AND THE RESTRICTED WAY

In Matthew 15 Jesus points out that there is another door, another way. It's distinct and different from the broad gate and the broad way all of us were born to travel. At first glance this alternative door—a small and unpretentious one—holds little intrinsic appeal. Not surprisingly, it opens upon a narrow, less-traveled path, little more than a dirt track in comparison to its broad counterpart.

In Matthew 7:14 Jesus explains a little more about this narrow gate. It's so small and inconspicuous that it's easy to miss. In the Christian classic *Pilgrim's Progress* John Bunyan envisions this gate as being so poorly marked as to be difficult to find; once discovered, the determined traveler has to bend over in order to squeeze through. The Greek word translated "narrow" is interesting, carrying the seemingly unrelated meanings of "restricted" and "afflicted." Jesus points out that this footpath will indeed be characterized by difficulty and affliction. Those negotiating the narrow way may even at times secretly wish for the amenities on the wide road.

The people traveling the narrow road appear different from the perspective of those on the wide road. As Henry David Thoreau reflected, "If a man does not keep pace with his companions, perhaps it is because he hears a different drummer. Let him step to the music which he hears, however measured or far away." The people on the narrow way have a different speech pattern, a different morality, and a different way of treating people. They recognize and value God, and they recognize and value people made in the image of God.

Some posit that people become Christians because they're weak and need a crutch or a wheelchair in order to get around. They see Christ and Christianity as a convenient prop to help those who can't make it through life on their own. The truth is, though, that the door Christ calls us to enter and the road he directs us to travel aren't for the faint of heart. Contrary to what many may think, the rutted path to which Christ beckons is difficult and fraught with afflictions. It's a road of self-denial and self-sacrifice. We'll look more closely at this in a later chapter in which we'll consider the cost of following Christ. The point here is that this choice is more pricey by far than even most Christians are aware.

Remember that passage way back there in Genesis 3, recounting how the door to life and purpose through Eden has forever been closed? Here Jesus whets our interest by asserting that God has provided a solution. Another portal has been created, another passageway opened. What Jesus doesn't tell us yet in Matthew 7 is precisely what or where that door is. He clues us in that it's small and warns us that navigating that road will be difficult. But we'll have to turn elsewhere to learn more.

The New Testament book of John points to an interesting progression in the life of Christ. John incorporates into his Gospel (his "good news" account) a number of statements that mesh with this idea of a new door and a new way. If what Scripture says about humanity's condition before God is accurate, we're born into this life with no adequacy within ourselves—nothing appropriate or effectual from our side that we can carry to God. We're born physically alive but spiritually lifeless, cut off with no sustaining umbilical cord stretching between ourselves and God. In order for God to open that new door *for us*, He has to do something different *in us*. We need a whole life transplant!

Several New Testament writers speak to the counterintuitive notion of new birth—that idea of being "born again." We do well to bear in mind that God's purposes will not be denied or thwarted. If God wants sons and daughters He will have them. The verses we're about to consider demonstrate this convincingly. Interested? Read on!

CHAPTER 8

BECOMING CHILDREN OF GOD

Already in Genesis 1 and 2, way back there "in the beginning," God was already creating children to build a family for Himself. In John 1:12 we see this thread of thought picked up: "To all who received Him he gave the right to become children of God." Notice how this ties in with the "narrow door" of the last chapter. One of the popular beliefs of travelers on the wide way is that "we are all God's children." In other words, God is good to all who seek Him, and any old path to finding Him will do. That's the cry of modern religious liberalism. God is often viewed as a benign presence who just wants to see His children happy.

C. S. Lewis describes this modern liberal mindset in the book *The Problem of Pain*:

By the goodness of God we mean nowadays almost exclusively His lovingness; and in this we may be right. And by Love, in this context, most of us mean kindness—the desire to see others than the self happy; not happy in this way or in that, but just happy. What would really satisfy us would be a God who said of anything we happened to like doing, "What does it matter so long as they are contented?" We want, in fact, not so much a Father in Heaven as a grandfather in heaven—a senile benevolence who, as they say, "liked to see young people enjoying themselves", and whose plan for the universe was simply that it might be truly said at the end of the day, "a good time was had by all". Not many people, I admit, would formulate a theology in precisely those terms: but a conception not very different lurks at the back of many minds. I do not claim to be an exception: I should very much like to live in a universe which was governed on such lines. But since it is abundantly clear that I don't, and since I have reason to believe, nevertheless, that God is Love, I conclude that my conception of love needs correction.

(C. S. Lewis, *The Problem of Pain*, chapter 3)

The God who created and loves us does so for our good and for His own glory. Just as parents need to have expectations of their children in order to guide them toward responsible adulthood, so God works within us to turn us into productive members of his kingdom.

Scripture makes clear that though we are all "creations" or "creatures of God" we are not all His sons or daughters. Becoming a child of God necessitates an extra step, one that involves receiving Jesus and integrating belief in His Son, as Savior, into our life.

John 1:12 needs a little explaining in that we have significantly altered its perceived meaning through misuse in the contemporary church. First, what does it mean to "receive" Jesus? The word "receive" is a somewhat weak translation of the Greek *lambano*, which contains the idea of taking hold of and appropriating something. Consider picking up a slice of bread and eating it. When a person "receives" Christ in the way the Bible writers intended, they're taking hold of Him and absorbing His life and work on their behalf into their own life.

Another word that needs to be revisited is the one commonly translated "believe" or "belief." To the modern mind "to believe" means accepting something as true in my mind, regardless or whether or not that affirmation will make any difference in my life. I may intellectually assent to or agree with the statement that George Washington was the first president of the United States, but that belief has no impact on my day-to-day life. My "believing in" George doesn't change my character or make me a significantly better person. Similarly, I can intellectually subscribe to the fact that Mohammed claimed to be a prophet, but this is not a life-changing reality for me. I simply agree with the stated proposition.

When John said "to those who believed . . ." he intended something much more profound. The Greek word can alternately be translated "belief," "faith," or "trust." Belief in the New Testament implies much more than intellectually agreeing with a proposition or idea. Believing in something or someone makes a difference in one's worldview, value system, and behavior. In the New Testament faith is always accompanied by action.

Let me provide a more contemporary example. The Wallenda family has been famous in circus circles for many years. They are known for aerial acrobatics such as trapeze acts and tightrope walking. In June of 2012 Nik Wallenda had a tightrope strung across Niagara Falls. His publicly stated intent was to walk across the falls. Several weeks of publicity preceded the event, which was televised nationally.

For the sake of illustration, let's say my wife and I are at Niagara Falls for several days leading up to the event. A week before the event I point out to her that the advertising states that Wallenda is going to walk a tightrope across the falls, and I ask my wife whether she believes he will do it. She says yes, that he would be a fool to say he could walk the rope and then not follow through. Let's say that a few days later we see another advertisement that claims Wallenda is going to walk a tightrope across the falls and take a wheelbarrow with him. I ask my wife whether she believes he'll do it, and she again says yes. Then on the day of the event we see an advertisement that says Wallenda is going to walk a tightrope across Niagara Falls with a wheelbarrow with a person in it. That evening my wife and I decide to attend the crossing. We observe Wallenda preparing to cross; he has the wheelbarrow up on the wire with him. At that point I tell my wife Wallenda is looking for a volunteer to cross with him in the wheelbarrow. Would she allow him to cross with her in it? If she does enter the wheelbarrow, she's demonstrating genuine faith.

Up to this point my wife has intellectually agreed with the notion that Wallenda can and will successfully walk over the falls. But not until she gets into the wheelbarrow has she exercised true belief or faith *in* Wallenda. Remember that the Greek word translated "belief" or "faith" includes the idea of trust. This is what John means when he speaks of believing in Jesus.

Let's examine one final word in this passage: "name." We moderns may name our children based on any number of criteria: personal preference, family tradition, the meaning of the name, a favorite actor or actress, a mentor or hero we want to honor, or a respected religious personality, to name only a few. Whatever the reason we select a given name, the idea or impetus behind the choice seldom moves beyond this surface consideration. This was not the case in Bible times.

In the Bible a name involved the description, or recognition, of a person's character—though we do wonder how a character trait would have been manifest in infancy! In some cases names were later changed—Simon to Peter, Saul to Paul.

The angel Gabriel announced the name of Jesus to His parents, directing Mary to so name her unborn son because He would save His people from their sins. The name Jesus is a translation of a translation; Jesus is a Latinized version of Jesus' Hebrew name. In the Greek His name was pronounced *Iesous*, but in the Hebrew, the language of His ancestry, His given name was "Yeshua." You might see a similarity here between "Yeshua" and "Joshua." Joshua is the rendering of the Hebrew directly into English without the intervening Greek and Latin renditions. *Yeshua* means "savior" or "deliverer" in the Hebrew language. Jesus' name embodied the work God had sent His Son to do.

We also need to look at "Christ." Again, this is a Greek rendering of a Hebrew word, *Meshiach*. An astute reader might make the connection with the word "messiah," meaning "anointed." When a person was set aside for service they were anointed with oil by a governing authority. "Christ" is not Jesus' last name or surname but a descriptive title. In the Old Testament God had promised that He would send a Savior uniquely appointed for the mission of raising up a new race of people for Himself. In New Testament times Jesus' disciples knew Him as *Yeshua ha Meshiach*: "Jesus the Anointed" or "Jesus the Christ."

Who anointed Jesus for service? In this case God Himself did the anointing. That was the purpose of Jesus' baptism by John the Baptist and the descent of the Holy Spirit upon Jesus in the form of a dove (Matthew 3:16). The baptism was the context in which God anointed Jesus for His work of delivering God's people from their sins. Jesus' name, then, literally means "Anointed Savior," embodying His mission and work. The anointing refers to God's act of publicly demonstrating that Jesus is His appointed person for the task of saving humanity.

Do you begin to see what John is saying here? When we receive and believe in Jesus, we take hold of Him and absorb both Him and His mission into our lives (or into ourselves). Our belief changes us from being creatures of the world to becoming children of God. John stated that Jesus gave the right to become children of God to those who would lay hold of Him and His work. And that process of taking hold of Jesus' name changes the direction of our lives because it entails altering our conduct to match His. Jesus becomes the example after which we model our lives. When we truly come to faith we're entrusting the future course of our lives to Him. We're putting our trust, faith, and confidence in the work Jesus came to do, and that faith changes the way we live, speak, and relate to others.

John addressed this issue again in 1 John 3:1: "See how great a love the Father has for us, that we should be called children of God; and such we are!" And in John 11:49–52, after Jesus had raised Lazarus from the dead, we read this account:

> But one of them, Caiaphas, who was high priest that year, said to them, "You know nothing at all, nor do you take into account that it is expedient for you that one man die for the people, and that the whole nation not perish." Now he did not say this on his own initiative, but being high priest that year, he prophesied that Jesus was going to die for the nation, and not for the nation only, but in order that He might also gather together into one the children of God who are scattered abroad.

The mention of "scattered" children of God points to us. For the past 2,000 years God has been gathering together His children from every nation, tribe, language group, and color, consistently building his kingdom with those who have dedicated their lives to him. In J. R. R. Tolkien's acclaimed *Lord of the Rings* trilogy there is a group of men known as Rangers. No one really knew who they were, nor did anyone trust them a great deal. In the end we learn that they constituted a lost race of kings who had hidden themselves among others until the time of their revealing and authority was to take place.

The concept of the "children of God scattered abroad" is similar. *We* are a hidden race of prophets, priests, and kings whom God is gathering together to rule His kingdom. Paul picks up this theme in Galatians 3:26: "For you are all sons of God through faith in Christ." And again in Romans 8:14: "For all who are being led by the Spirit of God, these are the sons of God." (The terms "children" and "sons" may be used interchangeably.) God is still in the process of fulfilling His original purpose of building a family. He still intends to have sons and daughters created uniquely in His image. God still intends to have us rule in the kingdom. But how, you may ask, is He going to bring this about?

CHAPTER 9

YOU MUST BE BORN AGAIN

J ohn provides the answer in several passages. In previous chapters we discussed the reality that all of us as humans come into this world as spiritual stillborns. If the old spirit with which we're born is dead to God, the only reasonable solution is that a new spirit must be implanted within us to replace the old one.

This concept of a spiritual birth is found in several New Testament passages. Some think of this as a rebirth, but in reality it's a new birth of an entirely different kind. A great place to begin our examination of this concept is John 3. In this account Jesus was approached by a man named Nicodemus. We know several facts about him from the passage.

First, he was a Jew with a Greek name. As the Greek culture spread throughout the Middle East, it became fashionable for wealthy and educated Jews to give Greek names to their children. Nicodemus's name indicates both that he was a product of contemporary Judaism and that he was a powerful man. The context indicates, in fact, that Nicodemus was a ruler of the Jews.

Second, we know he was a Pharisee, a highly educated religious person. Most people today have no idea how intelligent and well read these Pharisees were. Most had memorized the first five books of the Bible by the time they were five or six years old. They were brilliant students of the Hebrew Scriptures, our modern Old Testament, although many were misguided in their application of what they knew.

Remember that not all of the Pharisees were corrupt (though they were misguided, they were not necessarily intractable in terms of their positions). Both Nicodemus and the apostle Paul were Pharisees, and both later became powerful Christians. Paul was, in fact, preeminent among the Pharisees. Yet God's calling of this unlikely candidate enabled the process by which salvation came to all of us who were born outside the Jewish race and religion.

Third, we know Nicodemus was a ruler of the Jews, a man of wealth, power, and influence, well-known not only among the Jewish people but throughout the Jewish religious hierarchy. As such, he combined in his person religious knowledge and political power. One of the reasons he came to Jesus at night may well have been his desire not to be seen in conversation with Him; this influential man might have found it embarrassing to admit that his religion and knowledge were failing to satisfy the spiritual vacuum he felt within.

Fourth, we know that his religion wasn't satisfying to him. He came to Jesus with burning questions that couldn't be answered by the other religious people all around him. Nicodemus saw something different and intriguing in Jesus—a righteous man wielding power that could only have been given to Him by God—and Nicodemus wanted to know more. He also recognized that the power Jesus wielded wasn't available to the Jewish religious leadership. This influential Jewish leader had taken note of the miraculous works Jesus was performing, had heard Jesus teach, and recognized that God was at work in this man. All of these factors combined to cause Nicodemus to seek out Jesus for a private interview.

In Nicodemus we find a lesson for all of us. Religion in and of itself doesn't satisfy, the reason being that it doesn't satisfy the fundamental requirement God had in creating us: fellowship with Himself. Religion is an effort to placate God, to earn favor with the divine, to merit a place in heaven. Sadly, many people operate religiously, going through the motions of ritual and tradition without any sense of connection to or relationship with God. Ultimately, this sense is what Nicodemus was seeking.

Nicodemus's statement in John 3:2 reveals his recognition of the source of Jesus' power and teaching: "Rabbi, we know that you have come from God as a teacher; for no one can do these signs that You do unless God is with him." At this point he recognized Jesus as a teacher but did not yet acknowledge Him as anything more. Jesus responded with a comment designed to baffle Nicodemus and spur him to think more deeply. He informed Nicodemus that he had to be born a second time: "Truly, truly, I say to you, unless one is born again he cannot see the kingdom of God."

The word here translated "again" can carry an alternate meaning—"from above." Nicodemus evidently understood the word primarily in the more common first sense, prompting him to ask how a man could be born a second time. Jesus wasn't speaking of a second literal or physical birth, but Nicodemus didn't understand this. He might have thought Jesus was speaking nonsense but had too much respect for Him to indicate this perception.

In John 3:5–6 Jesus explains to Nicodemus that he must be born of the Spirit of God. In order for a man or woman to become a child of God, a new, spiritual birth has to take place. The life with which God infuses such a person can then grow toward God's purposes as the individual develops into the type of person to whom God will entrust His kingdom. The door that had slammed shut in Genesis 3, leaving us dead to God, has been reopened by Christ in the form of a new spirit instilled within an inert, lifeless body.

Years ago a saying was popular among younger Christians: "Born once, die twice. Born twice, die once." Do you catch the meaning? Those who are not born of the Spirit are twice dead. They were conceived and born spiritually dead (to God) and will die physically at the end of their temporal lives. The second death, spiritually speaking, is eternal separation from God in hell. In the Bible, death does not mean cessation of life. Death is the severance of a relationship. Whether we like it or not, all men and women are born with an eternal spirit. However, for the once born, biblically speaking, their spirit is dead to God. Once conceived, we will live forever. The only question is where forever will be spent.

However, those who are born of both the flesh and the Spirit only die once. The twice born will live forever with God in His eternal kingdom. Again, born once, die twice; born twice, die once.

In the Bible, and particularly in the New Testament, we're shown two different types of miracles. One is *restorative*. These are miracles of healing in which sight or hearing or some other physical ability is restored to someone who has lost it or was born with this faculty inoperative. Also included in this category are miracles in which disease is cured. The second type of miracle is *creative*. The obvious example is the creation of the world. In addition, Jesus turned water into wine and performed other creative acts. Of the two types, which do you think is the more significant? Most would say that creative miracles are more amazing and important.

In this passage Jesus is discussing a creative miracle. Any time a person becomes a child of God a new life is birthed within that person. God creates a new spirit by the power of his Holy Spirit and replaces the old spirit that was there. That individual then begins to grow and mature into a complete man or woman of God. This is the greatest of all miracles since the creation of the cosmos, since He is transforming someone who was to be condemned into someone who is to be loved, valued, and cherished forever as a child of God.

John 3 isn't the only passage in which John speaks of the issue of spiritual rebirth, nor is he the only New Testament writer to talk about being born again. In 1 John 5:1 he says, "Whoever believes that Jesus is the Christ is born of God, and whoever loves the Father loves the child born of Him." Belief in Jesus as the Christ is a sign that a person has become a Christian. It's important once again to understand that "belief" doesn't mean mere intellectual agreement. In the New Testament church "belief" or "faith" went much deeper than mental acceptance, signifying "trust in" or "reliance upon." Saving faith in the New Testament is a faith that alters the basic direction of one's life. True faith transports a man or woman to the narrow road.

In 1 Peter 1:3 Peter speaks of being born again to a living hope: "Blessed be the God and Father of our Lord Jesus Christ, who according to His great mercy caused us to be born again to a living hope through the resurrection of Jesus Christ from the dead." In our modern thought "hope" is a kind of vague desire for something we don't yet have—or know with certainty we'll get. In the Greek language the word translated "hope" literally means "earnest expectation." This expectation is based in solid, concrete evidence that what is hoped for will indeed be realized. Why can Christians "earnestly expect" or "hope" in a future resurrection that will reunite us with God? Because Jesus has been raised from the dead. As such, we have his promise that we too will be resurrected. We have been spiritually born again to a living hope. In verse 23 Peter goes on, "For you have been born again not of seed which is perishable but imperishable, that is, through the living and enduring word of God." Our spiritual birth is based in the understanding that God has spoken to us in the Scriptures and that He will always keep His Word and fulfill His promises.

To this point we have witnessed a closed door in Genesis 3 and an open door in Matthew 7. We have also seen from John 1 that God is bequeathing the right to become a child of God to men and women who believe in Jesus and that Jesus further characterizes this as in John 3 as a "new birth."

Many assume that the narrow way of which Jesus spoke in Matthew 7 refers to the ethic of the Sermon on the Mount. Certainly this is the ethic by which God wants His children to live. The requirements of the Sermon, though, go well beyond external obedience. God wants to be God of our thoughts as well as of our actions.

CHAPTER 10

A NEW DOOR OPENED

J esus carries forward the thought of the narrow door in Matthew 7 by identifying that door in John 10, where He relates the parable of the Good Shepherd. He distinguishes between a good shepherd and a thief, who comes only to steal and destroy the shepherd's flock. In contrast, when a shepherd puts his flock up at night he leads them into the pen through a single gate. The pen or corral represents a place of rest and safety for the sheep.

Unlike the open wilderness where they fed during the day, the pen is there to provide security through the dark night from wild animals and thieves. The sheep willingly enter the corral because they know and trust the shepherd. Jesus points out that the good shepherd, like the sheep, enters through the gate, while thieves try to sneak in by scaling the wall. When a shepherd has penned his flocks, it's customary for him to lie across the opening of the gate. The shepherd himself becomes the means of access to the pen or corral.

The pen in these verses represents the restfulness and safety afforded by kingdom citizenship. In verses 7–9 Jesus plainly identifies *Himself* as the door: "Truly, truly, I say to you, I am the door of the sheep. All who came before Me are thieves and robbers, but the sheep did not hear them. I am the door; if anyone enters through Me, he will be saved, and will go in and out and find pasture." In the Sermon on the Mount Jesus characterizes the narrow door and the narrow way to life by the principles laid out in the Sermon itself. Now He further identifies Himself as the narrow door. He is in fact both the "narrow door" and the pattern for life on the "narrow way."

CHAPTER 11

A NEW WAY

I n John 14:6 Jesus refers to Himself as "the way, the truth, and the life," going on, "No one comes to the Father except through Me." Notice that Jesus isn't calling Himself "another way, another truth, and another life." He is definitive in His statements: He is The Way; and there is no other. He is The Truth; and there is no higher truth. He is The Life; and there is no spiritual life apart from Him.

Peter reiterated this in Acts 4:12: "There is salvation in no one else; For there is no other name under heaven that has been given among men by which we must be saved." And Paul says this about Jesus: "There is one God, and one mediator also between God and men, the man Christ Jesus" (1 Timothy 2:5-6). The unanimous testimony of the New Testament writers is that Jesus has opened a new door and a new way back to fellowship with God and to kingdom citizenship. The door that was sealed shut by God because of Adam's sin has been replaced by a second door God has opened for us through Christ. In Christ we can once again realize God's purposes for us. We are put back on the path of fellowship with God as His children, placed again on the path to becoming his family on the earth, continuing the dominion with which Adam and Eve were charged.

Are you beginning to see where Christ is taking us? In Matthew 7 He directs us to enter through the narrow gate, but He doesn't tell us exactly what, or where, that gate is. Now Jesus informs us that *He* is the gate and that entrance into the kingdom of God lies through Him.

If the wide gate and the broad way are the truth, it doesn't make any difference which road you're traveling. However, if what Jesus says is true, if He is indeed the only door and the only way back to God, then every other road leads to destruction. A person can't lose anything on the narrow road, and he has everything to gain by traveling it. In contrast, the people on the broad road have nothing to gain and everything to lose. Because each person has been endowed with free will, each has the prerogative to accept or reject Jesus' teachings. If they choose to reject Jesus, however, they had better be very sure about their choice. An incorrect decision or unbelief would be eternally fatal.

Many people identify Jesus either as a great philosopher or as a good moral teacher. In his lovely little volume *Mere*

Christianity C. S. Lewis has the following to say—and it has been repeated many times since he wrote it: "A man who was merely a man and said the sort of things Jesus said would not be a great moral teacher. He would either be a lunatic on the level with a man who says he is a poached egg or he would be the devil of hell. You must make your choice. Either this was, and is, the Son of God, or else a madman or something much worse. You can shut Him up for a fool or you can fall at His feet and call Him Lord and God. But let us not come with any patronizing nonsense about His being a great human teacher. He has not left that open to us. He did not intend to."

PASCAL'S WAGER

Blaise Pascal was a French mathematician and philosopher who was also a Christian. Pascal is the person who pioneered the study of modern probability theory. In practical terms, in card games people might study the probability of a person being dealt two of a kind, three of a kind, a straight, a flush, and so on. Or in a game of dice, what are the odds that a person will roll doubles? The modern games of craps and poker are based on mathematical probability. Interestingly, the same is true of insurance. Insurance companies calculate how much to charge for life insurance based on what are called "mortality tables." They know within a minute fraction of a percentage point how many people in the general population will die at any given age. They can predict how many 21-year-olds will die in a given year, how many 22-year-olds, and so forth. They also know that the older we become the greater the odds that we will die. That's why insurance companies charge younger people lower rates than they do older people.

Based on his studies, Pascal designed a wager or bet concerning God. In his paradigm there are two possibilities: either God exists or He doesn't. Pascal further stated that there are two possible decisions people can make regarding these statements. Either a person can believe that God exists and live in light of that conclusion, or he can believe that God does not exist and live any way he chooses. At this juncture there are four possible outcomes. If a person believes that God does not exist, and it turns out God does not exist, that person gains nothing. If a person believes God exists, and God doesn't exist, he loses nothing. If a person chooses to believe that God doesn't exist, and God does exist, he loses everything. If the person believes that God exists, and it turns out God does in fact exist, the person gains everything. So the only reasonable wager is to believe God exists and then to act accordingly. None of the other bets has any potentially positive outcome.

Before we move on, let me ask you some questions. In terms of the journey of life, through which gate have you entered? Which way are you traveling? Have you received and believed in Jesus? Have you been born of the Spirit of God? Have you come to see Jesus as the Door? Have you entered into the narrow way with Him? If not, all you have to do is change course and answer the above questions with a yes.

CHAPTER 12

A NEW CREATION

To this point we have looked at the fact that God is continuing His plan of creating a family. There is a flow and a progression in the statement of Jesus and the apostles in the New Testament. In Matthew 7 Jesus speaks of a new or narrow gate. In John 1 John tell us that Jesus came to make children of God. In John 3 Jesus speaks to fact that becoming children of God involves the need to be born again (or born from above) spiritually. In John 10 Jesus says that He is the door. In John 14 Jesus identifies Himself as the Way, the Truth, and the Life. In the next few paragraphs we will see that Paul and Peter each pick up the theme of change and transformation, each in a different way. Paul will speak of a new creature or creation. Peter speaks of the change as a new race of people, a new kind if you will. We will look at the statements of Paul and Peter in the next few pages. If you take these statements to heart, you'll be absolutely amazed at what God is doing today and what He intends to do in the future.

A NEW CREATURE

In 2 Corinthians 5:17 Paul declares, "Therefore if anyone is in Christ, he is a new creature; the old things have passed away; behold, new things have come." Paul has been telling his Corinthian readers about the weaknesses and impending deaths of our physical bodies. Many Christians long to be released from their body and united with Christ. After death, we have the promise of a new body that is no longer subject to weakness, sickness, debility, or death. When we read about Christ's activity after the resurrection (see Mark 16 and John 21), we even have an example of what that new body will look like and be able to do. Many of our current physical limitations are going to be removed when God gives us our new bodies.

In Paul's thinking, a person's status here and now, in the flesh, is irrelevant. It makes no difference whether a man or woman is rich or poor, slave or free, white or black, or any other artificial distinction we've identified to differentiate ourselves. Paul points out that any person who is in Christ is a new creature. The Greek word he uses is *ktisis*, which can be translated either as "creature" or "creation." When a person comes to faith in Christ, when they're "born again," they become entirely different—a new creature in Christ.

A NEW CREATION

In Galatians 6:15 Paul writes, "For neither is circumcision anything, nor uncircumcision, but a new creation." Again, we need to look at the context. The book of Galatians addresses a significant issue in the New Testament church. Many of the early Jewish Christians believed that a Gentile (a non-Jew) had to adopt the Jewish practice of circumcision in order to become a Christian and join the church. The issue was so divisive that refusal to be circumcised sometimes led in the early church to persecution by Jews. Here Paul addresses the issue to correct the misunderstanding. In this context Paul writes that neither circumcision nor lack of circumcision is significant; the only thing that matters is "the new creation." In this verse the Greek word translated "creation" is the same one translated "creature" in 2 Corinthians 5:17. Once again it's the Greek *ktisis*, for which these alternative translations are interchangeable.

Are you recognizing the significance of what Paul is saying in these two verses? A person's old religious affiliations make no difference to Christ and shouldn't make a difference to those in the church. In Paul's thought neither Judaism nor any of the various pagan religions could bring a person into the kingdom of God. God had to do something new and different. Do you recall Jesus' words in John 3? Let's review: "Unless a man is born again [or born from above] he cannot

[even] see the kingdom of God." Judaism doesn't lead to kingdom citizenship, and neither does any other religion. The only thing that matters from God's perspective is a "spiritual birth" that translates into a "new creation" or that paves the way for one to become a "new creature."

For both Jesus and Paul, becoming a Christian involves something entirely new and different. If you're a Christian, a miracle of new life has taken place within you. The spirit that died to God in Adam has been replaced by a "new spirit" that is vital and alive to God. What an incredible thing God does in the life of a man, woman, or child he calls to be his own!

CHAPTER 13

A NEW NATIONAL IDENTITY

nother of the apostles approached the subject from a different angle. Peter wrote in 1 Peter 2:9, "But you are a Chosen Race, a Royal Priesthood, a Holy Nation, A people for God's own possession, so that you may proclaim the excellences of Him who called you out of darkness into His marvelous light." I want to focus on one word in this verse before returning a little later to the verse as a whole.

Peter referred to his readers as a "chosen race." The Greek word for race is *genos.* You may recognize some similarities between this word and some English words such as "gene," "genotype," or "genealogy." The word can also be translated "kind" in the sense of a particular type of organism.

Biological terms in English come from the Greek language. *Bio,* as we know, means "life," while *ology* derives from the Greek *logia,* "to study." Taken together, "biology" means the "study of life." Likewise, "herpetology" is a combination of *herpon*, which means creeping, and *logia*, which means study. Herpetology is the study of creeping things or reptiles. In biology various living things are categorized by "genotype," "genus," or "kind." We use these words to refer to a natural grouping of creatures—to a species. Generally speaking, things classified in a "genus" share similar characteristics and, with some exceptions, are able to reproduce. For example, while a mule shares most of the characteristics found in the equine or horse family, the ability to reproduce has been bred out. Cats, as felines, produce cats, and all cats, from lions and tigers to the tabby cat in your house, are related and part of the feline family. The same thing is true up and down the spectrum of genotypes or kinds in biology.

Why is a discussion of biology pertinent to the point the apostle is making in 1 Peter 2:9? Around 609 B.C. the Babylonians under Nebuchadnezzar swept through the Middle East and captured, among other people groups, the Jews. They led a large number of these captives back to Babylon and integrated them into the Babylonian population and culture. Most of the Jewish ruling class, both political and religious, were taken as exiled captives to Babylon. Men like Ezekiel, Daniel, Shadrach, Meshach, and Abednego were part of this group. They learned the Babylonian language and customs. Some, like Daniel, were assigned positions in government. Daniel so distinguished himself in his service that he was made a leader over one third of the realm.

The Jewish people were held in captivity for 70 years, after which many were allowed to return to their native Israel. The Old Testament books of Ezra and Nehemiah deal with the return of the exiles to Israel. Over a period of 70 years most of the original Jewish exiles had died. However, the faithful Jews had raised their children with the belief that they would someday be allowed to return to Israel, the land God had promised them by covenant with Abraham.

A group of the children and grandchildren of the original captives returned in 530 B.C., but they had lost much of their ability to understand the Hebrew language. For the most part they spoke Aramaic, the language of the Babylonians. Nearly 200 years later, Alexander the Great led the Greek armies east around the Mediterranean and through what is now the Middle East and North Africa. Alexander made Greek the official language of the ancient Middle East; as a result, the Hebrew language essentially vanished from all but the highly educated segments of religious Jewry.

The Jewish people could no longer read the ancient Scriptures in their original Hebrew language. The only solution was to create a Greek translation of the Old Testament the Jews could read. In about 270 B.C. approximately 70 Jewish scholars were contracted to create a Greek translation of the Old Testament that is still known as the *Septuagint,* meaning "seventy," after the 70 Jewish scholars who did the translation work.

Now for the punch line.

Genesis 1 is a description of God's creation of the universe, the world, and the living things He placed in the world. Ten times within 15 verses Moses writes that God created plants and animals that would reproduce after their "own kind." The Hebrew word is *min,* for which the Jewish scholars used the Greek *genos*—the same word Peter used that is here translated "race" in English.

The English "race" doesn't accurately represent what Peter intended to communicate. A better translation is "kind." Are you catching the ramifications in Peter's words "you are a chosen 'kind' or 'race'"? Peter is saying that Christians are a new "genus," a new "kind" of creature. He is repeating the thoughts of Jesus and Paul using slightly different words.

If a man or woman comes to Christ, he or she becomes a new creature, a new creation, a new kind or being: a child of God. For the Christian, life is changed. Something brand new and glorious is being put into place. The goal is now to live out the new life God has placed within us and to leave behind the old life—which is dead, gone, and irrelevant, meaningless to God and, by extension, to ourselves. The old physical distinctions we once possessed and used to differentiate ourselves from one another are inapplicable to the Christian's life. Nationalism is thrown out the window, and racism has no place within the church. Only the new life matters, because only the new life with which God has infused the Christian remains and will live forever.

CHAPTER 14

TWO ADAMS

I f you're having trouble coming to grips with what Peter is saying about a new race, take a look at Paul's words in 1 Corinthians 15, where he takes us back to Genesis and then forward again to Christ. Paul speaks of a first and second Adam.

In 1 Corinthians 15:21–22 the apostle wrote, "For since by a man came death, by a man also came the resurrection of the dead. For as in Adam all die, so also in Christ all will be made alive." In verse 45 Paul picks up the thought again with these words: "So also it is written, 'The first man, Adam, became a living soul.' The last Adam became a life-giving spirit."

Who was that first Adam? We've examined his life in our discussion of Genesis 1–3. He was the first human male, the founding father of our race. All of our genetic makeup comes from Adam and Eve. As an interesting aside, about 23 years ago an article appeared in the *Dallas Morning News* in Dallas,

Texas. The thesis was that DNA research had proven that all of humanity was descended from one woman. The scientists who came up with the data symbolically called her "Eve."

All that we are—body, mind/soul, and spirit—came from God to us through Adam and Eve. The first Adam came as a life-giving soul, "life-giving" in the sense that God endowed him and Eve with the ability to reproduce. However, because of his disobedience he was unable to convey the spiritual life of God to his offspring. In this sense Adam became a father of death to all who would be born in the human race.

In 1 Corinthians 15:22 Paul states, "As in Adam all die, so also in Christ all will be made alive." And in verse 45 the apostle refers to the last Adam, Christ, as a "life-giving spirit." Paul is making a connection we might easily have missed. Taken in context, he first offers proof of the resurrection, after which he introduces the idea of the same new race or "kind" to which Peter also referred to in 1 Peter 2:9.

From this we learn that Jesus is the founding father of a new race of beings called "children of God." The resurrection from the dead and into kingdom life belongs to those who are descended, spiritually speaking, from the second Adam. This concept of a new door, a new beginning, a new birth, and a new kind/race was integral to the early church's understanding of who they were in Christ. It provided the vision necessary to expand the church and enable the teaching of the gospel to transform lives and empower believers to endure persecution.

In large part the modern church has lost sight of this fact. We've confused kingdom citizenship with church membership, or with being a part of a particular denomination, or even with being a good person or some other foolishness along this line. We've adopted a country-club mentality with regard to church membership; we've even been led to believe that our particular country club is better than the others, which in turn has led to a smorgasbord of churches and denominations. Because we've lost sight of who and what we are in Christ, we've descended into nonsense and blindness. We've allowed ourselves to be caught up in all the same things on which the world is focused: power, position, seeking financial advantage by abusing relationships within the church, and on and on.

When I was in seminary John MacArthur spoke in out chapel services in a weeklong series of messages titled the Griffith Thomas lectures. One of the nuggets he conveyed to us 37 years ago was this: "The reason so many Christians think they are doing so well is because they don't know what they are doing." Has that ever proven to be true!

In light of the chaos we see in Christianity today, it's no wonder so many are confused or frustrated or have given up on the faith entirely. When my wife and I drive down certain streets in our hometown we can see as many as five or six churches within a couple of blocks of each other. If I were on the outside of the Christian faith looking in, I would think the whole system was nuts. If I'd come from a background with no church experience, and if I were looking for a church, I would be completely confused. Why are there so many churches? Which one should I attend? As often as not a person's choice of which to attend is based on some personal preference or subjective feeling. Can they take care of my children? Can this church put my marriage or life back together? Are the people approachable? Most of the time the decision of where to attend, if the choice is made to attend at all, is based on an egocentric perception of what this church can do *for* me or my family. When the current church for whatever reason no longer seems to fit the bill, such people simply church shop—and then hop.

Although this is hardly what Jesus intended, there are numerous reasons the various church groups have originated. Some are legitimate, but in my opinion most of the time churches divide because of some insignificant article of doctrine over which two groups disagree. Like the story of the feud between the Hatfields and the McCoys, most of us have forgotten what we were fighting over in the first place . . . if our history with the group with which we've affiliated even takes us back that far.

It's important for us to recognize that Jesus didn't die to establish a new religious group or denomination, to create Catholics, Methodists, Episcopalians, Baptists, the Church of Christ, Evangelical Bible Church people, or any other religious group. Nor did He die to establish his position as a moral reformer or ethical teacher—or even to make bad men good.

Here's the point: *Jesus died to make dead people live, to make it possible for men and women from every nation, tongue, tribe, and people group to become sons and daughters of God. Only those who are born spiritually into the Kingdom of God and accept it as their new nationality are truly children of God. Jesus died to open a second door back to Eden to replace the door that was locked up tight in Genesis 3. Jesus died to create a new kind of being, to make dead men and women alive to God.*

CHAPTER 15

GOD IS THINKING TRANSFORMATION

D o you see the progression in God's thoughts here? Along with Him, we move from condemnation in Adam to regeneration in Christ to transformation by the Holy Spirit.

In light of what Jesus and the apostles have to say about the true nature of the church, what should be the role of the local church in all of this? One of the things that distresses me most today is seeing pastors who look at their churches as their own personal kingdoms or fiefdoms. The church in this paradigm takes on the form of a charm school, a reform school, a mental/emotional hospital, a soup kitchen, or some other craziness. The same thing can be said about denominational hierarchies. So often these hierarchies morph into mini-kingdoms that need to be preserved for the benefit of the denominational leaders. Many have either forgotten, or have never seen, that they are supposed to be subsets and microcosms of the Kingdom of God. It is one of the great tragedies of contemporary Christianity, at least in the United States. I can't speak the rest of the world, but we have largely lost these truths in the American church today.

This is the reality: if you're a Christian, you're now a part of another race of beings. You're a child of God and a citizen of His kingdom. Your last name or position in the community is meaningless to God. Your racial heritage, gender, genetic makeup, psychological profile, or whatever else you or those around you use to identify you is extraneous to who you are in Christ and what He wants you to become.

God's goal is that the Christian be transformed into the image of Jesus and that each local church be a place that facilitates this transformation. If you want to know what you as a Christian are supposed to look like, look at the life of Christ in the Bible. Years ago my children sported bracelets with the acronym WWJD, standing for "What would Jesus do?" Jesus is the model or pattern God has established for us to emulate.

When I look at my six children I see various physical and behavioral traits they have inherited or learned from my wife and me. Sometimes I see my own dad or grandfather looking back at me in the mirror, and I see some of those same traits in our children. I also glimpse some of the genetic, physiological, emotional, and psychological characteristics of my wife's family in them. Each has a genetic imprint or stamp on their lives inherited from the conjunction of the two of us in our union.

Similarly, if you're a Christian you've inherited a spiritual, genetic imprint or stamp from God. The life He has caused to be birthed within you must be nurtured and fed and encouraged to become all God wants it to be. The greatest goal a Christian can set, the greatest good to which he or she can attain, is to be like our heavenly Father and our elder Brother, Jesus, whose imprint we carry.

Tragically, we've in large part lost our vision of who we are and what we can be in Christ. King Solomon pointed out in Proverbs 29:18 that without vision a people will perish or be unrestrained. Instead of being transformed into the image of Christ, the church in many of its iterations is being transformed into conformity with the world around it. In Christ's vision each local church is to be a microcosm, a miniature representation of the kingdom of God. Pastors and church leaders must always be seeking to be individually transformed into the image of Christ, and they should be actively engaged in helping their people achieve the same goal. If you're looking for a church home, this is the primary question you should be asking: "Can this church and its leadership help me achieve God's goal of looking more like Him and His Son?" If you can't find a church that aims at this objective, consider starting one that will do so. Instead of pursuing this objective, too many of us are substituting anything and everything else for our kingdom identity and purpose.

The early Christians and their churches understood that they were something different, a unique society separated from the world around it. The church of the first century had its own government and way of regulating itself. Its members' way of life was so evidently distinct from that of those around them that they attracted others into their circle. The early church took seriously Christ's statements that we are to function as salt and light (Matthew 5:13–16), and in so doing its members transformed the world around them.

Compare that dynamic to the situation in churches today that are running as hard as they can just to be accepted by the world around them. They assume that watering down the harder truths of the gospel makes them "seeker friendly," but they've taken this to such an extreme that they've rendered themselves virtually indistinguishable from the world. The world looks in on these church bodies and asks, "What's the difference between this church and any other well-intentioned, inspirational social institution?" When they aren't persuaded of its relevance Christ's church is diminished, and all too soon it becomes irrelevant.

It's time for a change. It's time to go back to our roots, both individually as Christians and corporately as a church.

What an incredible thing God has done for us! If you're a child of God, you're a living, breathing, walking miracle. What are you going to do with this truth? How now will you live? The New Testament writers give us some clues.

CHAPTER 16

FROM CONFORMATION TO TRANSFORMATION

HOW GOD CHANGES HIS PEOPLE

Most surveys and polls that deal with the larger questions of life conclude that people are looking for meaning, purpose, and identity. From the Builder Generation of the Depression era and World War II to the Baby Boomers and Generation Y kids (or whatever the latest generational identification marker is), the results show that people are looking for relevance and significance, as well as for solutions to the social and spiritual issues they face in their marriages, families, jobs, neighborhoods, and communities. In our search for meaning we've dabbled with psychology, sociology, anthropology, drugs, sex, and politics (probably the worst least productive avenue of all), to name only a few; and they've all left us hanging. Some purport that

Christianity has failed as well. I once heard a phrase, however, that puts this in perspective for me: "It's not so much that Biblical Christianity has been tried and it failed as it is that it has never truly been tried at all."

The ancient church made no attempt to be seeker friendly. The people in its ranks recognized that they were called to be a society set apart and that God had a unique goal for them. In my mind Paul's statement in Romans 12:1–2 could serve as the Magna Carta for the church (note: parenthetical explanations added): "I urge you therefore, brethren, by the mercies of God, to present your bodies a living and holy sacrifice, acceptable to God, which is your spiritual [or reasonable] service of worship. And do not be conformed to this world [literally, "age"], but be transformed by the renewing of your mind, so that you may prove [demonstrate] what the will of God is, that which is good and acceptable and perfect."

These verses are too important to pass by with a cursory glance. Once again we need to hone in on a handful of words in order to grasp Paul's intent, as well as to consider the context of Romans 9–11. Paul has spent three chapters talking about how God has brought the Gentiles, the non-Jewish peoples, into the kingdom of God. He has spoken of God's great love for us and the great works and sacrifices God has made to incorporate us into the family of faith.

First, Paul reminds us of our motive: "I urge you therefore, brethren, by the mercies of God . . ." God has gone to great lengths to enfold us into His family. He spared nothing to redeem us—so much so that He relinquished the most important thing in His life, a Person, His Son, as a sacrifice for sin so that sin would no longer pose an insurmountable barrier between people and God. The wall between us and God has been breached; His mercy is free to flow unabated. Gratitude and loving obedience constitute our only appropriate response. Our motivation in the Christian life is gratitude for what God has done, both for us and in us. God's mercy is our motivation for overflowing gratitude, as well as for allowing Him to continue to develop us, through His Spirit, in the direction of Christlikeness.

In the next few verses Paul delivers admonitions or exhortations. He tells us first that he wants us "to present our bodies a living and holy sacrifice." The word "present" means to offer up or to offer alongside. Paul wants us to present *ourselves* to God as living sacrifices.

By definition, someone who makes a sacrifice gives up something that is valuable to them, either in terms of possessions or of a life. Paul enjoins us to give our lives to God so that He can use them in whatever way He intended in the first place. We're to lay down our own lives in an offering of *service* to God. Many people today think the free offer of salvation means that God is giving everything to us with no reciprocal expectation. This is a tragic misunderstanding. God offered up the life of His Son in exchange for our lives. He offers us a trade.

The other significant point to recognize is that sacrifice is costly and painful. Either something of value has to be relinquished or something painful has to be endured. Doesn't this conform precisely to what Christ taught us about the narrow way? By way of reminder, the Greek word translated "narrow" can also mean "restricted" and "afflicted." The narrow way is a difficult and sometimes painful path to walk. It involves sacrifice—the living sacrifice of our bodies in God's service.

Next, Paul instructs us not to be "conformed to this world." The Greek word here rendered "conformed" is highly descriptive, meaning literally "to press into a mold." Think for a moment of Play-Doh®. It comes in small cans in a variety of colors. Children shape it into various things, or they can use molds—shaped as animals or objects—that come with a kit. A child can press the Play-Doh into the mold, and—*voila!*—out comes a piece of clay in the shape or form of the mold. The Play-Doh takes on the shape of, or is "conformed to," the mold. Paul is cautioning us not to allow ourselves to be pressed and shaped into the preset mold of this world.

What does the mold of the world look like? What, precisely, is it we're to be set apart from? John provides a definition in 1 John 2:16: "For all that is in the world, the lust of the flesh and the lust of the eyes and the boastful pride of life, is not from the Father, but is from the world." The world offers sensuality, fleshly indulgence, and false intellectualism, to name only a few of its attractions. As humans *in this world* we find ourselves so immersed in its "things" that we have a hard time stepping back far enough to get a vantage point for assessment. But Paul instructs us not even to take on the *appearance* of these things. He has another injunction for us.

Paul calls us to be *transformed*. Again his chosen Greek word, *metamorphizo*, is descriptive; you may recognize it as the root of the English "metamorphosis." When a dun-colored, hairy caterpillar enters a cocoon it undergoes a radical transformation, a change of appearance that will be revealed over time and with maturity. We too are to be metamorphosed or transformed into something that demonstrates all that is good and acceptable and perfect in the will of God. This process alters our personal character, which in turn transforms our marriage, family, and other relationships. We leave behind our old-life form and identity, taking on an entirely new form and look showcasing all that God has done for us and in us.

Paul goes on to tell us how we're to go about this transformation: by the "renewing of our minds." Two suggestions for implementing this process are spending time in God's Word and sitting under the instruction of gifted teachers of that Word. The purpose isn't to cram our notebooks and heads with new information but to allow newfound knowledge to shape our thoughts and actions. Seeking God's power for transformation through prayer and in reliance on the Spirit is another way of renewing our minds. Finally, spending time with fellow travelers on the narrow way is a significant help.

CHAPTER 17

ROI

Transformation as a process begins in the present. God is using the current circumstances in the world and in our lives to shape, mold, and strengthen us, His children, so we can become all He wants us to be. We can take only two things with us into that final phase of eternity with God: (1) the character we've developed, or that God has developed in us, and (2) the people we've influenced along the way.

I spent several years in the investment business; my job was to take clients' dollars and place them in investments that would offer attractive rates of return to grow their savings. Through this experience I learned that there is no such thing in this life as a safe investment: all are subject to risk. That being the case, wouldn't it be wise for us to make our investments of time, talent, and treasure in that which *is* failsafe? Only two things last forever: God's Word and God's people. These are the only eternal investments, the *only* two entities that guarantee a great—no, an *infinite*—return.

Our investment in God's Word transforms us into the likeness of Christ. Think of the Bible as an owner's manual similar to the one you would find in a car. The manual in the glove compartment of a new vehicle tells you everything you'll need to know in order to maintain it in peak operating condition. It tells you what type of gasoline to purchase, what type of oil the car needs, how frequently the oil needs to be changed, and so forth. The same is true for the Christian of the Bible. It's God's owner's manual telling us how to live. God designed His book in part to show us how to be all He wants us to be.

Our investment in God's people is the second asset Jesus informs us will last forever: "And I say to you, make friends for yourselves by means of the wealth of unrighteousness, so that when it fails, they may welcome you into the eternal dwellings" (Luke 16:9). In the context, Jesus is directing us to use our earthly resources to build relationships that will last forever. He's pointing out that some of the people we either lead to Him or assist with growing in Him will precede us in death. They'll be waiting for us on the other side to welcome and thank us for the contributions we've made to their lives.

ROI is a business acronym meaning "Return on Investment." When a business person invests money or capital in his own or another company, he looks at how much money he's likely to earn or has already earned as a result of the investment—the rate of growth in his capital. But the idea of return on investment originated not from human thought but from God.

It's important to realize that God expects a return on His investment *in us*. Many professing Christians in the modern American church believe that if they pray a prayer or walk an aisle and profess their faith in Jesus, nothing more will be demanded or expected from them. Much of modern evangelism focuses on incenting people to declare faith in Jesus. But Jesus makes it abundantly clear that He isn't interested in people making "decisions." He *is* interested in their becoming disciples. The Greek word for disciple means "learner"; as such, a disciple is a student who has committed himself or herself to a teacher for the purpose of emulating the teacher.

Jesus' early disciples did more than cram in order to pass a test. A disciple was someone who learned with the purpose of imitating the teacher. Jesus isn't primarily interested in people who want to fill notebooks with the goal of passing a test. He's interested in people who've been equipped by His example and empowered by His Spirit to realize their full potential in God's eyes. From God's perspective, a decision to follow Jesus is just the starting point. The end goal is a mature

Christian who not only looks like His Son but can be trusted with leadership in His kingdom.

Remember the original premise: God is the eternal King of the universe who rules over an eternal kingdom. He is currently populating His kingdom with an eternal race He calls His children and to whom He intends to entrust the rule of that kingdom. God won't entrust His riches to foolish, lazy, or ignorant people. The process begins in this life, not the next.

Much of today's church has also lost sight of the fact that, although no one can merit salvation on the basis of his or her good deeds (we know this fallacious concept as "works righteousness"), God *will reward* His children based on their obedience to Him and their fruitfulness as a result of that obedience. Some examples from the life of Christ should convince the reader of this fact:

In Matthew 25 Jesus presents us with the parable of the talents. A talent was a large sum of money, based on its weight. A Greek talent of silver weighed 82 ¼ pounds, while a Hebrew talent of silver weighed 94 3/7 pounds(Typesetter, can these other fractions be set like "¼," above?). A gold talent was double the weight of a silver talent. In this illustration a gold talent would have weighed 188 6/7 pounds. For the sake of discussion let's assume the master was using gold talents. As of the writing of this book, the price of gold is around

$1,382 per ounce and has during the past year been as high as $1,700 per ounce. We'll use the current figure and assume the Hebrew weight of 188 6/7 pounds per talent. This would equal around 3,022 ounces of gold. In today's market that equates to an estimated value of $4,176,010 per talent of gold!

The master in the parable entrusted five talents of gold to one servant, two to a second, and one to a third; the amount consigned to each servant was based on the master's opinion of his ability to manage the investment. However, whether a servant was given five talents or one, the calculations above demonstrate that the trust was significant. The first and second servants invested the gold and doubled its value. The third, based on his risk aversion and defeatist attitude, didn't even bother to invest the gold. He buried it in the ground and then simply returned the original amount back to the master when he returned; he hadn't even bothered to deposit the gold in a bank account where it could at least have earned some modest interest.

When the master returned he called in the servants to settle accounts. He rewarded the faithfulness of the first two with greatly expanded responsibilities in his business. In case you haven't made the connection, in this parable the Master's business is the kingdom of God. The unfaithfulness of the third servant was punished by expulsion, resulting in a life of torment and regret. The point is that God expects faithfulness from His people, a return on the investment He has entrusted to them. You can't separate faithfulness from service. In Scripture faith isn't simply an intellectual exercise but an action word.

In Matthew's Gospel, chapter 21, we find the story of Jesus and the fig tree. The reader should understand that this tree was symbolic of the nation of Israel, a nation God had established from one man, Abraham, 2,000 years earlier. There are a number of references in the Old Testament informing us that God intended for Israel to be a nation of kings and priests. Israel was to be God's outreach center to the rest of the world, but the leaders and priests had failed to understand and, hence, to carry out their mission. The nation was unfruitful.

Jesus approached the fig tree, ostensibly expecting to find fruit to eat, even though we're informed that it wasn't the season for figs. In response, Jesus cursed the tree, which immediately withered and died. Not long afterward Jesus pronounced judgment on the Jews and Israel for their failure to live up to God's requirements and expectations for His people. In 70 A.D. the Romans invaded Israel, the temple was destroyed, and the Jewish people were again dispersed throughout the world. They remained a displaced people until May 15, 1948, when they reentered and recaptured the land and formed the modern state of Israel.

Jesus expects fruitfulness, a return on His investment in His people. The example of the Jews alerts us that failing to bear fruit is something we as Christians want to avoid. As a result, we need to examine what fruitfulness looks like from Jesus' perspective.

CHAPTER 18

GOD'S EXPECTATION OF FRUITFULNESS

There are two kinds of fruit mentioned in Scripture, fruit we'll refer to as "attitude" fruit and "action" fruit. We'll look at each in turn.

ATTITUDE FRUIT

The first kind of fruit God wants to produce in us might be called "attitude" fruit. In Galatians 5:22–23 Paul tells us that "the fruit of the Spirit is love, joy, peace, patience, kindness, goodness, faithfulness, gentleness, self-control; against such things there is no law." Most of us recognize and desire such things. Why, then, does "attitude" fruit come first? The answer lies in the necessity of attitude preceding action. If we think and feel rightly, we'll usually do what's right. I think most of us would like to see this fruit produced in our lives.

I know very few people who don't want to be loving, joyful, peaceful, and the like.

How often, though, doesn't the fruit of the Spirit seem to elude us? I can look back to too many times in my own life when I've cried out to God for this fruit, only to have my cries seem to bounce off the ceiling. However, I'm learning some things about fruitfulness that may be helpful to you, as they've been to me. I believe we need to remember two things.

First, the Holy Spirit is the One who produces fruit in our lives. We can't generate it by our own efforts. An apple tree doesn't strain and groan to pop out an apple; it bears fruit because it's in its nature to do so. Jesus addresses this issue in John 15, the story of the vine and the vinedresser. Cultivating a vineyard was a common farming operation in Jesus' time. The branch of a grapevine produces grapes simply by remaining attached to the plant's main stem or trunk. In Jesus' analogy He is the vine and His followers its branches. Jesus instructs us to "abide" or "remain" in Him. As we do so, as we communicate with Him and rely on the Spirit to enable us to live God-honoring lives, He produces in us the fruit of the Spirit. In this passage Jesus makes it abundantly clear that our responsibility is to remain in and rely upon the Spirit to bear His fruit in us. From many years of experience with Christ I can tell you that hanging on to the vine may be more difficult than it sounds. Read on to learn why.

John 15 also speaks of an aspect of fruit bearing we don't necessarily want to hear about. Jesus talks about God as a vinedresser who prunes the branches of the vine to cause it to produce more fruit. Pruning involves cutting off dead and weak branches from a vine or fruit tree in order to allow more moisture and nutrients to reach the remaining branches. Anyone who has ever tended fruit trees or vineyards is intimately familiar with this process. If a fruit tree or vine had nerve endings or emotional attachments, it would probably find the pruning process to be excruciating. If Jesus is at work to mature you, you too have a lot of compromised branches—aspects of your life that are unproductive for Him. These areas of unproductivity and deadness need to be cut or pruned away. The process can be painful, but it's necessary, once again, if you're going to reach your optimal potential as God's child and heir of the promises given in Christ.

In raising children we call this process "discipline," and God, through the inspired author of Hebrews, uses the same term: "Whom the Lord loves, He disciplines, and He scourges every son whom He receives" (Hebrews 12:6). The Greek word translated "scourges" refers to a severe beating; this is the same word used in the Gospels for the beating Pontius Pilate ordered for Jesus just before the crucifixion. The process can seem agonizing, but God deems it necessary in order for us to produce the fruit He has a right to expect.

Second, the development or ripening of fruit is less than instantaneous. We have apple, peach, and cherry trees in our backyard. Every year we prune, fertilize, and water them. And every spring they, in their turn, put out blossoms and leaves, but it takes two or three months for those blossoms to become mature fruit. In fact, the process of producing a successful fruit crop begins shortly after the previous harvest. Pruning, watering, and fertilizing entail a year-round process, and every year the tree itself grows a little bigger and produces more fruit. The ups and downs of life, coupled with knowledge of God's Word and reliance upon His Spirit, translate into ever-enhanced fruitfulness.

ACTION FRUIT

The second variety of fruit we'll call "action" fruit. In Ephesians 5:9 Paul enjoins us to "walk as children of Light (for the fruit of the Light *consists* in all goodness and righteousness and truth) trying to learn what is pleasing to the Lord." Many Christians have memorized Ephesians 2:8–9: "For by grace are you saved through faith, and that not of yourselves; it is the gift of God, not as a result of works, lest anyone should boast." Verse 10 is the explanation of what God does in verses 8 and 9: "For we are His [God's] workmanship, created in Christ Jesus for good works which God prepared beforehand, that we should walk in them."

God wants us to do good in His name. Goodness, righteousness, and truth grow out of correct attitudes and translate into the good things we do for others around us—and ultimately for God. This may look like spending time with someone who is going through difficult circumstances. It may mean giving money to someone who is desperately in need, or encouraging someone who is being systematically beaten down by life. Each person we encounter has a unique set of needs and problems, and each situation demands a targeted, appropriate response. The truth is that, whenever we encounter a need, we also meet an opportunity to do something good for that person in the name of Jesus. And when we do good to and for others we advance God's kingdom in the world, one life, one hurt, one need at a time.

Action fruit also leads to others coming to faith in Christ, often without the knowledge of the servant who came to their aid. Christians tend to look at evangelism in one of two ways: either as the only real fruit God wants or else as someone else's job—after which they ignore it entirely. This latter group finds talking about Christ to unchurched friends or strangers difficult and uncomfortable. Yet biblical evangelism is as natural as an apple tree bearing apples. Most often it simply involves sharing what God has done in one's life with someone who is facing a similar difficult situation.

Imagine close friends confiding in you about a marital problem. They're distressed about the condition of their marriage and are looking for help. You have a solid marriage and can share with them the guidelines Jesus has given for fostering a healthy spousal relationship. Or perhaps your own marriage has struggled but God has helped you push through to a position of love and peace with your spouse. In either circumstance you share with that troubled couple what God has done for you. You can also share ways in which God's Holy Spirit has given you power to love your spouse even when you didn't feel like it. That's what a witness does. He or she relates their personal experience to others. Through that sharing others are influenced to follow Christ.

Let's look at a second example. Perhaps a friend comes and talks to you about problems he is having with his children. Anyone who has raised children has had problems. You can talk with him/her about their problem. You can identify with them, empathize with them, laugh, weep, etc. As time goes by you can share what God has taught you and how He has helped you in the raising or children. You can relate biblical principles for raising children and how God has worked in your family to enable you and your children to be all that God wants them to be. That is the living way to interest people in coming to faith in Jesus. That is attitude and action fruit at work.

The reason so many professing Christians have trouble in this area is that they themselves aren't living life in submission to the King. You simply can't share or give away what you don't have. It's difficult to talk to another person about how to keep a marriage together if your own marriage is in shambles.

Whenever the subject of talking to others about Jesus comes up, people run and hide. We've been taught artificial, awkward, and counterintuitive ways to communicate our faith. In reality, talking to another person about Jesus is no different from talking to them about other relationships in our lives. The real issue is whether or not you've established a relationship with Jesus that has transformed your life. If you have, your only honorable response is humble gratitude for what God has done in your life and a compulsion to share your experience with others in need. In Peter's words, "always [be] ready to make a defense to everyone who asks you to give an account for the hope that is in you" (1 Peter 3:15).

CHAPTER 19

A NEW PURPOSE

Two of the best-selling Christian books over the past 15 years, other than the Bible, are *The Purpose Driven Life* and *The Purpose Driven Church*, both by Rick Warren, pastor of Saddleback Church in Lake Forest, California. The fact that these books have sold so many copies tells me that even those who regularly attend church are starving for some sense of identity, meaning, and purpose—something they aren't finding in their local churches. This is tragic because God has graced us with the most important purpose we can possibly have. For whatever reason many local churches are failing to teach this, or to help us as individuals to identify meaningful opportunities to fulfill the purposes God has for us.

Earlier I spoke of this in the context of God creating a new "kind" or "race" of being. Peter had this to say: "But you are a chosen race, a royal priesthood, a Holy Nation, a people for God's own possession, so that you may proclaim the excellences of Him who called you out of darkness into His marvelous light" (1 Peter 2:9). I also indicated that we would come back to this verse, . . . and here we are.

The truths in this verse are reinforced in other New Testament passages, and I want to expand on them here. Notice that all of these descriptions are in the present tense, referring to the now, not the later. While it's true that we aren't yet completed or mature, this description already describes who and what we are. And God is continuously working in us to make us more and more mature in these areas.

CHOSEN RACE

Peter first describes us as a "chosen" race, from the Greek *eklektos*. You may recognize the related English words "eclectic" and "elect." "Eclectic" is defined as "selecting what appears to be best in various doctrines, methods or styles. Composed of elements drawn from various sources" (quoted from the Merriam Webster Dictionary on line). Imbedded in the word is the idea of choice or selection. The New Testament writers make clear that God is in the business of adopting children from every nation, tribe, and language group. All over the world today people are coming by the millions to faith in Christ, and the rate of conversion in what Americans refer to as the Third World is in fact accelerating.

The word "elect," indicating choice, carries the idea of voting for or selecting a candidate. Peter refers to Christians as a "chosen" race. When God brought us into His family, He actively chose us, as individuals, out of all the peoples on the earth. Why, we ask, did He choose any one of us? Why, for example, did God choose *me*? Of one fact we can be sure: God's choice doesn't flow from anything in me. In fact, biblically speaking, *nothing* good dwells in me apart from Christ. Nothing. Nada. At all.

Our only available explanation for God's selection process is that He makes choices for reasons known only to Himself. He sovereignly chooses whomever He will because He wants to. There's nothing intrinsic in any of us that God needs. He chose you and me based on His good pleasure. How are we to respond to this? If He has elected *us* to be His children and destined us to rule with His Son in the kingdom of God, our only legitimate hindsight response is to fall on our faces with thanks and worship. We who know ourselves to be His ought to be the most humbly grateful people on the face of the earth. God has chosen, of His own sovereign will, to do something *for* us, *in* us, and *through* us, based on no merit of our own. If you're in Christ, you're a living, breathing, walking, talking miracle. That's the best and most profound of all reasons for us to fall on our faces in worship and to offer up in response our humble and grateful obedience.

ROYAL PRIESTHOOD

Peter moves on to describe us as a "royal priesthood." At first this seems like a disconnect. Royalty rules and priests serve. However, we see from the Old Testament that God originally intended to govern the Jews through the Levitical priesthood. They constituted, in truth, a *royal priesthood*. If this is what we are, it's important for us to know what functions the priests carried out so we can imitate them. We know from the Old Testament that priests interceded and offered sacrifices. Let's look at each of these functions.

INTERCESSION

Priests also interceded for the people. This means that they stood as go-betweens or mediators between God and the populace to pray for the people. In Numbers 21:7 we observe the people coming to Moses; they had sinned against God and were asking him to intercede, or step in, between themselves and God, asking God to forgive them. In Romans 8:26 Paul beautifully depicts the Holy Spirit as interceding for us with groans and utterances too deep for human words or comprehension. And in Hebrews 7:25 the author notes that Jesus is seated at the right hand of God, *always living* to make intercession for us.

If I'm a Christian, then I'm a royal priest. Just who is it for whom God wants me to intercede? Certainly we all have unbelieving friends, neighbors, and relatives. We're to approach God on their behalf, asking Him to open their hearts and grant us the opportunity to initiate the process of winning them to a faith that will culminate in the Spirit's working in their lives.

A major movement today is in the area of called prayer evangelism represented by the "Houses of Prayer" movement. After visiting with their unchurched neighbors and soliciting their prayer requests, small groups of Christians gather in neighborhoods all around the country to pray. The only stipulation the Christians are placing on their neighbors is that they advise them when the prayers are answered. As the uninitiated see evidence of God answering prayer, they want to know more about Christ.

We can also intercede on behalf of others who are experiencing spiritual warfare. In 2 Corinthians 4:4 Paul writes, "In whose case the god of this world has blinded the minds of the unbelieving so that they might not see the light of the gospel of the glory of Christ, who is the image of God." In 1 Timothy 4:1 Paul writes, "But the Spirit explicitly says that in the later times some will fall away from the faith, paying attention to deceitful spirits and the doctrines of demons." Paul is saying that people are spiritually blinded by Satan, the god of this world, and evil spirits who carry out his bidding. We can beseech God to bind the spirits and open the spiritual eyes of those for whom we're praying. In the past sixteen months, as of my completion of this book, I have participated in evangelistic crusades in South America five times—four in South Africa and one in my home city here in the United States. After each message we've invite people forward for prayer, healing, and to be set free from this evil influence. On each occasion I've witnessed men, women, and children being delivered from demonic possession or influence based on the intercessory prayers of pastors and Christian leaders.

An elderly friend of mine here in town is grappling with failing health. Yet God has given her a ministry of intercessory prayer unlike any I've seen before. The leadership of our church regularly sends people from the congregation to her so she will pray for them.

This friend, Dorothy, has had me on her prayer list for many years. In October of 2012 I was in Bogota, Colombia, for a series of meetings in the church of a close friend. At 5:00 in the morning I was taking a shower to prepare for my day at the church when I suddenly felt weak and cold. I could barely lift my arms and wasn't sure what was happening to me. At the same time—at 5:00 a.m. while I was in the shower experiencing this weakness—Dorothy was awakened by God with the urgent injunction to pray for me. Sensing that I was under demonic attack, she interceded with God on my behalf. As both of us, 2,500 miles apart, were entreating

God about the same event, the attack and its corresponding weakness simply disappeared.

These are just a few examples of how God can use each of us as His delegated priests to intercede with Him on behalf of others.

SACRIFICES

Another function of priests is to offer sacrifices. In the Old Testament priests sacrificed animals, as well as grain and oil, on the people's behalf. In our age the church isn't asked to offer animal sacrifices. Christ has already provided the once-for-all-time blood sacrifice necessary for us to be forgiven and cleansed from sin before God. However, there are other aspects of sacrifice in which we're called to engage.

In Romans 12:1 Paul urged his readers to offer their bodies as "living sacrifices"—in essence relinquishing their focus on earthly and fleshly pleasures to offer their lives to God in grateful obedience. This wasn't something new; Paul was restating what Jesus Himself had enjoined in the Gospels: in Matthew 16:24, "If anyone wishes to come after Me, he must deny Himself, and take up his cross and follow Me," and in Luke 14:27, "Whoever does not carry his own cross and come after Me cannot be My disciple." In Galatians 2:20 Paul reinforced our Lord's injunction, along with our beautiful motivation to follow it: "I have been crucified with

Christ; it is no longer I who live, but Christ lives in me, and the life I now live in the flesh I live by faith in the Son of God who loved me and gave Himself up for me."

We offer ourselves as a sacrifice to God when we sacrifice our time, talents, and treasure for the kingdom cause, when we set aside our personal desires, ambitions, and passions for the sake of knowing Jesus and making Him known. Ours is not a race for recognition or power but an inner, love-induced compulsion to lay down our lives so that others might live. When I was in seminary the late Dr. Howard Hendricks told us this: "Gentlemen, you are not going into the ministry to make a name. You are going into the ministry to serve a Name." Along with John the Baptist we are to adopt the attitude that "He [Jesus] must increase, but I must decrease" (John 3:30). We as believer priests ought to continually be laying down our lives so that others might rise.

HOLY NATION

Peter goes on to describe God's family as a "holy nation." The Greek word here rendered "holy" means "separate," "set apart," or "distinct." The word translated "nation" is *ethnos*, from which you may recognize the English "ethnic," which according to the *Theological Dictionary of the New Testament* describes a "'mass' or 'host' or 'multitude' bound by the same manners, customs, or other distinctive features." The church is bound together by a common faith in Jesus Christ and as such is committed to carrying out the mandates of the faith given to us both by Christ Himself and by the apostles. Unlike the nations of the world, which are bound together by language, geography, or both, the church is an altogether different entity: it knows no geographic boundaries and it has no single common language except that of the Word and of the Spirit.

However, just as surely as we are a new "race" or "kind," we are also a distinct nation. Furthermore, we are a separate culture. All countries have their own unique customs and cultures. In working in other cultures I have encountered problems in relating to others due to misunderstanding what a phrase or action might imply. The church is not to acculturate, or take on the customs, of the surrounding peoples. (By this I don't mean that we aren't to use certain styles of worship or recognize certain customs of other countries. For example, if I were to visit a church in Africa or Latin America, I would expect to worship in African or Latin style. I would also expect to honor some of their interpersonal customs.) God has a culture designated for the church, and it's defined in many places in The New Testament.

Peter goes on to help us understand what he means by "a holy nation" in verse 11: "Beloved, I urge you as aliens and strangers to abstain from fleshly lusts which wage war against the soul." Think back a couple of verses to his reference to Christians as "a chosen race." Here Peter refers to us as "aliens and strangers." If we're truly in Christ we're no longer, spiritually speaking, citizens of this world. We're citizens of the kingdom of God, and our obedience and allegiance are to His kingdom.

Knowing what we do of jurisdictions, it should come as no surprise that in God's kingdom the rules are different. For one thing, we're to abstain from the fleshly lusts that war within us. To eliminate any misunderstanding, Paul lists the elements—the attitudes and actions—motivated by the "flesh" (our inborn sin nature) in Galatians 5:19–21: "Now the deeds of the flesh are evident, which are: immorality, impurity, sensuality, idolatry, sorcery, enmities, strife, jealousy, outbursts of anger, disputes, dissensions, factions, envying, drunkenness, carousing, and things like these, of which I forewarn you, just as I have forewarned you, that those who practice such things will not inherit the kingdom of God." In a negative sense, we are a holy nation in that we abstain from the fleshly actions and fixations spoken of by Paul. In a positive sense, we have good works to do, and we experience the benefits and rewards of obedience in our health, marriages, families, and relationships within the church, to name only a few.

In one sense the adjective Peter uses to describe this nation, the people of God, is what distinguishes or defines us:

we are a "holy" nation, a nation "set apart" as distinct from all others of the world by our common faith in Christ and our commitment to being unique in our speech and behavior. To cite some practical ramifications, we aren't consumed with self-interest but take an active interest in the well-being of those around us. We don't join in or affiliate with the philosophic trends of the world. We endeavor to stimulate one another to love and good deeds. We're a holy nation in that we aren't disposed to emulate what the world considers good but instead commit ourselves to living in a manner *God* defines as good.

A PEOPLE FOR GOD'S OWN POSSESSION

The fourth descriptor Peter uses to define our character and standing is that we're a "people for God's own possession." This touches our lives at a much more personal level. The concept appears two other times in the New Testament, both in the letters of Paul. In Ephesians 1:13–14 Paul writes, "In Him, you also, after listening to the message of truth, the gospel of your salvation—having also believed, you were sealed in Him with the Holy Spirit of promise, who is given as a pledge of our inheritance, with a view to the redemption of *God's own* possession, to the praise of His glory." And in Titus 2:14 the apostle describes Jesus Christ as One "who gave Himself for us to redeem us from every lawless deed, and to purify for Himself a people for His own possession, zealous for good deeds."

That word translated "redemption" is interesting in the Greek, carrying the idea of releasing someone or something in response to the payment of a ransom. A couple of illustrations may help. When I was a child stores offered "Green Stamps" as an early type of loyalty rewards program. When a person spent money at the grocery store or filled the gas tank, they were given Green Stamps as a kind of thank-you. The number of stamps given was proportionate to the amount of money spent. Books were also supplied in which to glue the stamps. There was another store in town that accepted Green Stamps as currency. A shopper could bring in the filled or partially filled books and "purchase" merchandise with them at this "redemption center," the price commensurate with the amount of "currency" proffered via the books. When the merchandise was "redeemed," ownership transferred from the store to the purchaser.

Another picture of redemption is what we know as ransom. Kidnappers offer to release a captive upon receipt of a specified sum of money we know as a ransom payment. The payment purchases the hostage's freedom, "redeeming" her from captivity. Upon release the person is returned to her rightful "owners"—those who have paid her ransom.

Scripture makes clear that Jesus Christ came to offer His life as a ransom in order to buy back Christians from their slavery to sin. Who is holding the unsaved or unredeemed person hostage? They're being held by Satan and by sin. When Jesus gave His life on the cross, He was paying a ransom to redeem people from captivity and deliver them into God's possession. Spiritually speaking, a change of ownership takes place: the "child" of sin and Satan becomes the dearly loved son or daughter of God, the possession (in terms of loving entitlement and protection) of God Himself.

Note that Peter refers to us as "a people for God's own possession." From God's perspective, as well as our own, this is intensely personal. Are you beginning to see the progression? This change in possession carries with it a change in relationship. The redeemed person who believes in and receives Christ, who is born again of God's Spirit, is transformed through adoption into a child of God.

Recall with me that, from God's perspective, this is all about His building a family, about creating a "race" of children for His own possession, delight, and glory. Out of all the people who live or have lived throughout the history of the world, God has handpicked a select group to be His own.

If you're a true Christian, by extension *you* belong to God. In fact, you personally, out of all the people on the earth, are a part of His inheritance. If you're not yet a Christian, you might want to look at this book and this moment as an opportunity to reconsider your life choices. In a very real way the message of this book provides an opportunity for you to see what God has done and to ask Him to make you one of His children. You can choose to remain where and as you are, or you can choose to become God's child—a newly minted member of His family and kingdom. How does one go about doing this? By recognizing your need and crying out to God for His grace in adopting you. Adoption as God's child is a gift freely offered by God to anyone who asks for it.

Now to the issue of purpose. What is our only appropriate response to all that God has done for us? Peter defines for us what is to be our reason for living: "that you might proclaim the excellences of Him who called you out of darkness into His marvelous light." Each of us who has come to faith in Christ and adoption as God's child ought to respond in several ways. We should first be overwhelmed by God's love and provision for us, a response that calls us first to fall on our faces in gratitude and then to lift our hands and voices in praise and worship. We're to be so completely amazed by the effort God has expended to make us His children that we can't help but proclaim the excellence of that One who has given so much in order to give us even more! His excellencies are proclaimed to us and through us in worship within the church—as well as by us in gratitude to anyone who will listen.

CHAPTER 20

A NEW RACE OF GOVERNING PRIESTS

O ur theme in this book all along has been that God is the eternal King of the universe who rules over an everlasting kingdom. At one time in eternity past His kingdom was populated solely by marvelous beings we know as angels. In Adam and Eve God started a different program: He created people in His own image and likeness with whom He could have a Father/child relationship, to whom He could entrust the future governance of His kingdom, and from whom He could glean delight and receive glorification.

Some have asked me what God's endgame is to be. The answer is that the endgame is identical to the game as it was at its inception. God hasn't set aside the plan He put into place with Adam and Eve. In fact, that plan continues to unfold day by day as God continues to populate His kingdom with children in whom He has instilled a new Spirit. The Old and New Testament prophets all foresaw this. Now you will have an opportunity to glimpse what it was they saw.

In the Old Testament there were three preeminent prophets who experienced visions of the kingdom of God: Isaiah, Ezekiel, and Daniel. Each of these men had strikingly clear visions of the kingdom. Others saw it as well, but none more clearly than Daniel. Daniel 7 contains an incredible vision of the future that pertains directly to the church today.

In this chapter Daniel envisioned four great hybrid beasts emerging from the sea. One looked like a lion with the wings of an eagle, the second like a bear with ribs protruding from between its teeth, the third like a leopard with four wings, and the fourth a winged beast with four heads. The fourth beast is not described as resembling any other single beast, but its four faces do incorporate elements of the other three. Time and space do not allow for an exhaustive treatment of the prophecy, but suffice it to say that the beasts are representative of four nations that were either in existence at the time of Daniel's vision or due to come into existence within that time period to rule the Middle Eastern world. The lion was the city of Babylon (from the country of Babylonia), which ruled at the time of Daniel's vision. The bear was the Medo-Persian Empire, which was to succeed the Babylonians (think of the book of Esther). The leopard represented Greece, and the fourth beast typified Rome at the time of Christ. This God-sent vision and its interpretation afford us a rare window into heaven. Read on.

Daniel foresaw that the fourth beast would wage war against the saints—in other words, against God's people—but that the saints would eventually prevail. In Daniel 7:18 the prophet foretells: "But the saints of the Highest One will receive the kingdom and possess the kingdom forever, for all ages to come." Remember way back to the discussion on Genesis 1 where we're told that we were intended from our creation to ultimately rule the earth. Approximately 3,400 years later Daniel experienced his vision clarifying that God's purposes would (and still will!) be realized at a future date. In verse 27 Daniel predicts, "'Then the sovereignty, the dominion and the greatness of *all* the kingdoms under the whole heaven will be given to the people of the saints of the Highest One; His kingdom *will be* an everlasting kingdom, and all the dominions will serve and obey Him.'"

This message was very much a part of the good news (the meaning of the word "gospel") shared by Jesus and the apostles in the New Testament. The apostle Paul had himself planted the church in Corinth, and the Corinthian Christians constituted an interesting—and in some sense problematic—blending of spiritual gifts, fleshly indulgence, and pride. Paul wrote this letter to address the problems in that church.

In 1 Corinthians 4:8 Paul rebukes the spiritual pride of the believers there: "You are already filled, you have already become rich, you have become kings without us; and indeed, *I* wish that you had become kings so that we also might reign with you." My focal point here is the last part of the verse. Paul states, somewhat sarcastically, it would seem, that "you have become kings without us." Obviously these Christians had not yet become kings because the church wasn't ruling the earth. Still, at the end of the verse Paul is unable to refrain from adding a personal postscript that is both cryptic and wistful: "And indeed, I wish that you had become kings so that we also might reign with you." Encapsulated already within the early teachings of the church was the fact that the Christian community would someday rule the earth.

A few more Scripture verses reinforce this case. In 2 Timothy 2:12 Paul wrote, "If we endure, we will also reign with Him; If we deny Him, He also will deny us." In other words, God will reward our faithful endurance in the face of suffering with positions of authority in His kingdom.

And again in 1 Corinthians 6:3 Paul informs his readers that, incredibly, we will someday judge angels. In the courtroom, the judge is the ultimate authority. Yet we're told that in the kingdom of God *we* will stand in positions of authority over angels. When you examine from the scriptural record some of the tasks God uses the angels to accomplish, you'll realize that we're going to be entrusted with incredible power and authority in the future iteration of the kingdom.

Earlier in this book we discussed the parable of the talents. The servants who invested well and increased their master's net worth were rewarded with positions of authority over his property or holdings. Jesus gave us this parable to illustrate what He intends to do with us. The reward for our faithful obedience will be positions of authority in the kingdom of God. And with that great responsibility will come great power to fulfill the duties of our office.

There's a false belief in a kind of Christian Socialism within the church today. Karl Marx popularized a saying: "From each according to his ability, to each according to his need." The idea was that the government should redistribute a portion of the wealth of those who had produced a surplus by giving it to those who had incurred a deficit. The outcome of Socialism is evident around the world: it has universally failed (and will fail in the United States) because it punishes hard work and productivity and rewards either laziness or carelessness. If I work hard only to have what I produce taken away and given to someone else who declines to work, why should I exert myself? It's only natural that those of us who work do so with an eye toward the wage or the reward.

Socialism relies on an unbiblical view both of work and of the kingdom. Acts 2 provides an example of voluntary giving within the church, a phenomenon that occurred in its very early days. Later Paul made a course correction by stating that people who didn't work shouldn't be allowed to eat. There were some, even in those early days, who thought they could sponge off the church. Socialism attempts to redistribute wealth in a sort of Robin Hood politics where the government takes what is rightfully earned by some and hands it over to others who haven't done anything to earn it. God doesn't commend this anywhere in Scripture. Certainly salvation is the free gift of God, but our position in the kingdom is predicated upon faithful obedience and works that advance the kingdom. God is the One who incentivizes us to work, even for Him.

Following are some other verses in the book of Revelation on the related subjects of faithfulness and reigning with Christ:

"He who overcomes, and he who keeps My deeds until the end, to him I will give authority over the *nations* (Revelation 2:26).

"He who overcomes, I will grant to him to sit down with Me on My throne, as I also overcame and sat down with My Father on His throne" (Revelation 3:21). (Those who sit on thrones are in positions of power and authority. We will join Christ on His throne of governance, which is also joined to the throne of God the Father.)

"You have made them *to be* a kingdom and priests to our God; and they will reign upon the earth" (Revelation 5:10).

"Then I saw thrones, and they sat on them, and judgment was given to them. And I *saw* the souls of those who had been beheaded because of their testimony of Jesus and because of the word of God, and those who had not worshiped the beast or his image, and had not received the mark on their forehead and on their hand; and they came to life and reigned with Christ for a thousand years" (Revelation 20:4).

"Blessed and holy is the one who has a part in the first resurrection; over these the second death has no power, but they will be priests of God and of Christ and will reign with Him for a thousand years" (Revelation 20:6).

God hasn't given up on His plans and purposes for us. The present age with all of its difficulties and suffering is essential to our development into people to whom God can entrust His kingdom. We learn obedience through suffering.

Even Jesus learned obedience in this fashion. In Hebrews 5:8 the writer states that "although [Jesus] was a Son, He learned obedience from the things which He suffered." Please don't gloss over or underestimate this pronouncement. Jesus endured temptation, persecution, and all of the other trials we experience in this life. In Hebrews 4:15 the author declares, "For we do not have a high priest who cannot sympathize with our weakness, but One who has been tempted in all things as we are, yet without sin." Jesus in His human nature experienced all the hard stuff we do: rejection, misunderstanding, persecution, temptation, and the list goes on. If you're struggling under a load of despair, bear in mind that Jesus endured the same thing. He did so voluntarily, because this was necessary for His mission, and now you as a Christian are going through the trials of life because they're necessary for the mission God has called you to undertake.

No one can lead without knowing how to follow. Obedience isn't easy. Most of us don't like it and resist doing it. We want to do things our way and afterward ask God to either bless the results of our efforts or deliver us from the consequences of our disobedience. We want the end product without having to go through the process. Yet the process is absolutely essential to forming us into the rulers God wants us to be. Like Jesus, we're learning obedience through the things we suffer.

In Revelation we encounter another Tree of Life, though we don't find here a tree of the knowledge of good and evil.

Why? Because the children of the King already know good and evil. Revelation 22:5 speaks of our God-fueled reality in the coming kingdom: "there will no longer be *any* night; and they will not have need of the light of a lamp nor the light of the sun, because the Lord God will illumine them; and they will reign forever and ever."

In the end God wins. And the church, the children of God, will win with Him. That's the certain destiny God sets before His people. That's what God had in mind when He created us in His image and likeness, and that's still His thought process today (see Revelation 22:5, from the very the last chapter of the Bible). From beginning to end God is building an eternal family through whom He intends to rule the earth. We're destined to reign with Christ.

CHAPTER 21

THE GREAT OPPORTUNITY AND THE GREAT WAGER

n today's business world entrepreneurs are men and women who are innovators and developers of business. They generate the ideas, develop the plans, and invest the capital necessary to turn ideas into marketable realities. For the most part they're the risk takers in business. If they succeed they can often amass a lot of money and gain a lot of prestige. If they fail they often lose both fortune (or potential fortune) and status.

In a real sense God is the ultimate risk taker. He created people in His image and likeness, one aspect of which is the ability to exercise free choice, an attribute God also possesses. As long as it's consistent with His character, God can do anything and everything He desires, and He has imparted this attribute to us as well, despite our finite nature and inherent limitations. Would the two realities—finiteness and freedom—mesh? Would the outcome be positive?

True freedom of choice by definition includes the ability to choose that which is contrary to the will of God. When God created Adam and Eve, He placed two trees in the garden to develop their character and to provide them an opportunity to walk with Him in voluntary obedience. God was developing our fore-parents into the kind of people in whom He could invest ever-increasing amounts of power and authority. But the power had to be imparted over time.

Responsibility without authority is foolishness, while authority without responsibility leads to tyranny. For God to have entrusted unlimited authority to naïve and undisciplined men and women would have been disastrous. It didn't take long for Adam and Eve to make the wrong choices, plunging themselves, and by extension the entire human race, into the chaos we see around us today.

But Adam's unfortunate choice didn't cause God to abandon His plan. In a very real way, the circumstances and vicissitudes we experience in our daily life are part and parcel of that plan. If God knows everything, both actual and possible (and He does!), He foreknew before the creation how things were going to turn out. Further, if He is all-powerful (and He is), He could have created the world in such a way as to achieve any result He wanted. While creating in the way

He chose, He knew exactly how human history was going to progress. The sovereign Creator wasn't caught by surprise in Eden, nor is He being blindsided today.

Once again, its helps to bear in mind God's goal to make us like His Son. In Colossians 1:15 Paul tell us that Jesus Christ "is the image of the invisible God, the firstborn of all creation." And in Hebrews 1:3 the author speaks of Christ as "the radiance of [God's] glory and the exact representation of His nature," who "upholds all things by the word of His power." Jesus Himself declared that "he who has seen Me has seen the Father" (John 14:9). God is busy at work transforming us, little by little, into the image of His Son. If you want to know what God is like, set your gaze on Jesus. Again, if you question what God is transforming us to look like, focus on Jesus.

To give you an idea of the magnitude of the power we will one day wield, consider the angels as depicted in Scripture—beings of incredible power. In Isaiah 6 they cry out with voices so loud that they shake the foundations of the temple of God. They control wind and waves. They do battle in the invisible spirit world with the enemy forces of Satan. In nearly every incidence in Scripture in which angels appear to humans, people fall on their faces in awe, in fear, and at times, mistakenly, even in worship. In 1 Corinthians 6:3 Paul asks, "Do you not know that we will judge angels?" Who is more powerful, the person being judged or the judge?

Do you begin to see the incredible opportunity and promise God has placed at our disposal? Do you also recognize the incredible risk He is taking? One day in heaven we will have free choice combined with incredible power and authority. What's to keep us from rebelling?

In eternity past there was only one will in the universe, that of God. All was harmonious, peaceful, and joyful. But at some point another will asserted itself, that of Lucifer, whom we know as Satan. Lucifer longed for the worship and adoration all the creatures of the kingdom of God were directing toward God. Desiring what rightfully belonged to God, he revolted, leading one third of the host of heaven to rebel with him. Already then, prior to the creation, peace and harmony had been disrupted. This reality is clear from Ezekiel 28, which cannot simply refer to the creation account in the early chapters of Genesis. These verses can only refer to another spiritual reality that existed in eternity past, before time as we know it had come into existence.

It was only later that God created humans, who themselves revolted in the garden. As completed people in the kingdom of God we'll one day be able to grasp in retrospect what happens when more than one will is operative in the universe. We'll recognize that there can only be one will in the kingdom of God—and that this will can only be God's.

We aren't God—for which we can be eternally grateful to Him!—and our own wills can't and won't prevail.

Remember that God-fueled reality we'll experience, according to Revelation 22:5. In loving obedience, based on our recognition of what God has done for us and in us, we'll freely follow His leadership, reigning forever and ever in perfect harmony with His will. This will be the culmination of the incredible risk God is taking with us in the here and now. This is why He so painstakingly works with us and in us to conform us to the image of Christ in this life: He's making us fit to be His sons and daughters, equipping us in every way to rule in His kingdom. He's giving us the ultimate gift, including the right—at least in the here and now—to reject it. How can we help but marvel with John, "See how great a love the Father has for us, that we should be called children of God" (1 John 3:1)?

CHAPTER 22

WHAT WILL YOU DO WITH WHAT GOD HAS DONE FOR YOU?

Are you beginning to see the significance of what God is up to? In 1 Corinthians 2 Paul spoke of the simple message of Christ crucified and the measureless wisdom of God in His work among us. What God had done had been hidden or undisclosed in previous ages but was and is now being revealed to and through the church. Paul called this the "hidden wisdom" of God. In verse 9 he declares:

"But just as it is written,

'Things which eye has not seen and ear has not heard,

And *which* have not entered the heart of man,

All that God has prepared for those who love Him.'"

In light of what we've seen with regard to God's thinking, purposes, and plans for His people, there are some additional issues that need to be explored, some questions still to be asked and answered. First, what are we going to do with this information? How will we respond?

Many professed Christians haven't got a clue as to what God has been doing for and in them. They think the Christian life is all about attending church or doing nice things for others. They lack a basic understanding that God is at work transforming them into the image of His Son. My prayer has been, and will continue to be, that God will use this work to open blind eyes to catch a glimpse of that work. My hope is that this knowledge will transform the church from the weak, listless—and perhaps in some cases even lifeless—organization it is today into the living, breathing, power-infused entity God intends it to be.

It's time to wake up and live out our position in Christ.

For the unchurched or unsaved person reading this, my prayer is that you'll catch sight of a different version of Christ and Christianity from the one to which you've been exposed. Much of what you may have rejected—if you've made a conscious decision in one direction or the other—is probably also being rejected by Christ Himself. However, you can choose to follow Christ and look to Him for a transformed life suffused with the meaning and purpose that can only be found in walking with Him. As He begins to transform your life, you too will be used by His Spirit as an agent of transformation to those around you.

There's an interesting story I've shared many times. The theology is a little shaky, but the punch line is spot on. A man died and got on the elevator that would take him to his eternal resting place. The elevator operator asked him which direction he wanted to go—heaven or hell. The man thought about this for a minute and then reflected to the operator that this was a significant decision. He thought it only fair to look at both places before he made a final decision, since he was going to be spending eternity in his destination of choice. The elevator operator rejoined, "Fine, just remember that all decisions are final and irreversible. Once the decision is made there's no turning back." The operator then asked the man which direction he wanted to go first.

The man recalled that he had heard nothing but bad things about hell and felt it might be wise to get the bad news out of the way first. The elevator operator reiterated his earlier comment: "Fine, but just remember that all decisions are final and irreversible. Once you've made your choice there's no turning back."

The elevator descended to hell. When the doors opened, the man stepped out to survey the scene. To his surprise, hell was nothing like he'd been told. There was no visible fire, no brimstone, no demons with pitchforks, no weeping and wailing and gnashing of teeth. Instead, it was as though he had entered the center of a beach party, complete with wine, gorgeous women, gourmet food, volleyball, a pristine beach, and crashing waves—everything conceivable to delight a man.

The operator asked him what he thought, and the man responded that hell looked pretty good to him. However, to be thorough and fair, he ought to at least take a look at heaven. The operator repeated his refrain, after which the elevator ascended to heaven, the doors opened, and the man stepped out to a pleasant pastoral setting. Gazing around him, he took note of a gentle breeze, soft music, and people in white robes talking amongst themselves. The man surveyed the scene and concluded that this too would be nice. But there was no beach party or beautiful women or any of the other attractions he'd seen in hell.

Turning to the operator, he informed him that he'd made his decision—to spend eternity in hell. One last time the elevator operator repeated his cautionary words: "Fine, just remember that all decisions are final and irreversible. Once you've made your decision, there's no turning back." The man agreed and asked the operator to take him to hell.

The elevator descended and, when it reached its destination, the doors opened. But the scene had changed. Now the man did see the fire, feel the heat, and smell the sulfur and brimstone. He cried out to the operator: "Wait a minute. It wasn't like this before down here. Where are the beautiful women? Where's the beach party? Where's the wine and food that were here before?" To which the operator matter-of-factly responded. "Oh, you must have seen our promotional package."

The world and the devil know all too well how to bait a hook, but the reality is always far less than what they promise. The world, the flesh, and the devil invariably over-promise . . . and always under-deliver.

Someone somewhere has reflected that God and Christianity aren't realities man could create if he would, or would create if he could. The focus of our world's natural thought process is on the wide gate and the broad way. Why would anyone choose the narrow gate and the restricted way? Why even conceive of such a thing? The wide way is indeed replete with promised pleasures, but most have found them unfulfilling. That's because the world, the flesh, and the devil are liars and cheats. In the end, what was supposed to bring pleasure and meaning leaves only emptiness, poverty, destruction, and death. The Bible's entire emphasis runs counter to what most men and women think they want. The narrow way could only have been conceived of and brought into existence through the intervention of an outside force: the One the Scriptures refer to as God Almighty.

We only get one shot at life, so we have to get it right this time around. All decisions regarding Jesus are final and irrevocable. Think of what one single sin, one isolated act of disobedience, did to the human race. All Adam and Eve did was take a bite from a piece of forbidden fruit. They didn't commit adultery or murder, didn't steal or rape, didn't lie or defame anyone. They just took a taste test—which plunged the entire race of humanity into darkness, frustration, meaninglessness, and chaos.

One single act of biting into a piece of forbidden fruit, and all hell broke loose. The door to life in Eden was slammed shut, along with the opportunities that had been open for Adam: sonship and governance of the kingdom under God's delegation and leadership. But Jesus informs us that an alternate door has been opened, one that leads back to what God had originally intended for the human race. Can you imagine how God is going to respond if we reject His gracious offer to bring us back into relationship with Himself and restore us to our original purposes? If the message of Christ and the apostles is true, the results of such a negative choice will be devastating and catastrophic.

What in the world was God thinking when He put all of this into motion? While we can't presume to know God's thoughts, it's clear from Scripture that He had in mind and at heart a race of beings He could uniquely call sons and daughters, a family in which He could take delight, from which He could receive glorification, and to which He could entrust the governance of His kingdom. Because God is almighty and omniscient, He knew exactly what was going to happen when He created the world and set everything in motion. The evil and the good were both part of the plan.

Why, you may ask again, would God have done this? Why would He permit—or perhaps even design into the system—the whole convoluted situation we see today? The fact is that the current circumstances are vital to the process of building men and women into the image and likeness of God the Father, God the Son, and God the Holy Spirit. The current world situation constitutes the forge or smelting pot God is using to shape and refine His family.

Because God is changeless, we know that what He was thinking in Genesis is precisely the same as what He is thinking today. In Genesis 1 He created a race that could and did fall. In Revelation we see a redeemed race of people in restored fellowship with God and living out His purposes for humankind. We've seen that the New Testament closes in the book of Revelation gazing at the panorama that is the completed process: an incredible city overlooks a world governed by Jesus Christ and those who have responded to His call to enter through the narrow door, to be born from above, and to traipse the narrow way. The citizens of the kingdom are a new creative work of God who are allowing Him to transform them into the image and likeness of His only begotten (uncreated) Son.

Consider whether the things of this world you're grasping so tenaciously are so important that you can't bring yourself to leave them behind to become all God wants for you. What could so powerfully distract you that you wouldn't want to take God up on His offer, or to at least consider it very carefully before walking the other way?

The offer God is holding out to us staggers the imagination, and the stakes are unimaginably high. As I've reflected earlier, those on the narrow road can't lose, while those on the wide road stand to lose everything, forever.

CHAPTER 23

CONCLUSION

What are you going to do with the information you've been given in this book? How will you apply it in your life?

Remember that God wants to transform you into the image of His Son. What God was thinking when He created Adam and Eve is what He is still thinking today, and in the Revelation of Jesus Christ to John we see the same thing. In Genesis 1 we observe God creating a race of people in His image and likeness. Then in Revelation 22 we see the process completed with the people of God living in unbroken fellowship with God in the kingdom.

God is omniscient, knowing everything, both actual and possible. He is also omnipotent or almighty. He can do anything and everything, the only proviso being that it must be consistent with His character. When God fashioned and generated the cosmos he had already foreseen everything that would and will happen. He hasn't been caught by surprise at the fallout from the fall.

If this is the case, why did He set our world in motion? The answer is that this was the best possible way for God to transform His children into His image so that He could one day entrust the governance of that very kingdom to them.

You can live under the guidance and discipline of the great King, who is also your Father, and allow Him to shape you into what He wants you to be, or you can revolt and go your own way. In heaven people look to God and cry out "Your will be done." In hell God looks down at men who have refused His gracious offer and says to them "*Your* will be done."

EPILOGUE

I have several prayers in conjunction with this book. I've written it as an offering to Him—an offering with which I truly hope He is satisfied. It's the product of twenty years of thought, Bible study, and prayer. I hope and pray it's pleasing to Him and that He'll put His hand of blessing on it.

I hope and pray, too, that God will use this volume to provide a context for Christians that is to a large extent missing and badly needed in the church today. When a person becomes a Christian he or she is too often welcomed into the church but then left alone to figure out the Christian life. Even the best of educational programs often constitutes no more than a series of how to's: How to pray, how to share Christ, how to live, etc. God has so much more in mind for us—in terms both of a process and of a finished product. I hope this book will help you see both and enable you to fit your Bible Study, prayer, and worship into a total context for Christian living.

I pray that God in his grace will use the teachings offered here to place before us a vision for pressing on in the Christian life and becoming all God wants us to be. It's easy to become discouraged. If you haven't yet been disappointed by something or someone in the church, it's only a matter of time before you will be. There may even be times when you want to give up and throw in the towel, times when you wonder whether any of the promises of the Christian life are true. Remember that the process of discovery in which you're now engaged is vital to the ultimate outcome.

For my unchurched and unbelieving friends, I pray this book will provide a basis for thought and prayer that will lead you to trust Christ and walk the narrow way with Him. I understand where many of you are coming from. If all I saw was the nonsense you may have seen in the church, I'd be sorely tempted to walk away. But I've seen something entirely different: a minority who are on the narrow way, suffused with the fruit of God's Spirit, and committed to being all God has in mind and heart for them. They're an incredibly fun and inspiring group of men and women with whom to be associated. If you'd care to join me on the journey, perhaps I can even introduce you to some of them. I hope you'll find me to be one of them.

In the name of Jesus, the Christ, I invite you to join with me and my narrow circle of friends as we seek, by the grace and power of God, to be all He has called us to be. As God is my witness, it will be worth whatever price He calls us to pay.

Kirk Hartness
October 2014

ACKNOWLEDGMENTS

In the course of reliving my story while preparing my manuscript for publication I have come yet again to recognize those special individuals to whom I owe debts of gratitude I can never repay. All of them have deeply etched their influence upon my life by offering tremendous support and encouragement, even and perhaps especially during my most difficult times. I would be gravely remiss not to mention these individuals by name.

My wife, Barbara, who has endured more than anyone should reasonably expect over the years and who has been a continuous source of encouragement.

Dr. Warren Bathke, a man who graciously adopted me more than twenty years ago to be his mentee and friend. His wisdom, advice, and encouragement have left me deeply in his debt. In so many ways he has been a father to me, teaching me in incredible and indelible ways about life and ministry. I could only wish I had met him twenty years earlier.

Dr. William G. Swindell. In Proverbs 18:24 Solomon wrote, "A man of too many friends comes to ruin, but there is a friend who sticks closer than a brother." Bill is such a man, and his support has been so very important to me.

Sam Campbell. This companion has gone to be with the Lord, but I can never repay his kindness and encouragement through some troubled seasons of my life. He gave me perspective when I desperately needed it.

Dr. Wayne Kellogg. In addition to his encouragement and support, Wayne has contributed significantly to the publication of this work; a large measure of the credit goes to him.

To each of you goes my deepest affection and gratitude. This work would not have been possible without you.

ABOUT THE AUTHOR

 **KIRK HARTNESS** is an ordained pastor and a businessman with many years of experience in both pastoral ministry and business. He has a BS from the University of Central Missouri and a ThM from Dallas Theological Seminary. He has resided in Northwest Arkansas for many years, where he has worked as a pastor and as president of Peregrine Consulting Services, Inc.

Kirk is known among his friends as a man of integrity, with a prophetic passion to see people come to Christ and grow in Christ. His great passion is to see individual Christians and churches reinvigorated with a new vision of who they really are in Christ and what God is doing to transform them into the individuals and institutions He wants them to be.

Kirk is available for speaking engagements and consulting work with churches who use his book, *What in the World Was God Thinking?* as a springboard for church renewal and outreach.

He can be contacted by email at kirkhartness@gmail.com or through his website kirklhartness.com.

Rich Fleem
Dehher
Tim Ross
Not Smean
Big Onl — by chem
gurnl day clile
gurnl arr

J. B. Hunt